Rh
and Kos

with the Dodecanese Islands

Jarrold Publishing

CONTENTS

Kamiros

Introducing Rhodes and Kos

The islands of the Aegean fall into two categories: either barren and bare or luxuriant and green. It is a matter of personal preference which type you find most appealing.

The Dodecanese islands of Rhodes and Kos are both of the green variety — soft, pleasant and inviting. The Greek poet Pindar named Rhodes 'the child of Aphrodite' in praise of its beauty, and the playwright Irondas highlighted the fertility of Kos: 'It is good to live on sweet Kos, surrounded by the sea.'

Rhodes and Kos are sister islands. They are geographical neighbours and geologically related, and they share a similar history and culture. Owing to their strategic position off the coast of Asia Minor, they have been much coveted and fought over from prehistoric times until this century, for political, military and economic reasons. Since 1947 both islands have belonged to Greece. The latest invaders on Rhodes and Kos are the tourists, this time not because Rhodes and Kos are important places, but simply on account of their beauty. Those who adore sun, beaches or art are in their element.

From May until October there is sunshine and a cloudless sky. This is true of many southern shores, but the gods gave Rhodes two other heavenly gifts, water and wind. Whoever has travelled around Greece and other Greek islands in April or

May knows that in spring everything is in full bloom. However, the splendour is short-lived; the harvest is brought in during July, and under the scorching rays of the sun the earth dries out, breaks up and crumbles. The arrows of the sun god are deadly. Desert winds blow and the vegetation dies. Many of the Greek islands are without natural sources of water, and life is only possible with the help of large cisterns in which water has been collected during the winter. For the visitor, to be offered a glass of water as a welcoming drink is to be offered the most valuable commodity.

Rhodes and Kos are quite different. The islands are in the same latitude as North Africa, but the temperatures are bearable even in high summer. This is due to the *Meltemi*, a north-west wind which blows with the constancy of the trade winds, keeping things cool, turning countless windmills and occasionally making the sea crossing to Rhodes an eventful one.

'There is something exciting about planning a trip to Rhodes, because you are never quite certain of reaching the island.' This assertion by a clergyman named Toster is not even a hundred years old. It was correct for a long time, but today it is completely untrue. Almost every ship calls in at Rhodes and every day there are several direct flights from Athens, taking just over an hour, not to mention the countless charter flights direct to Rhodes. The same is true of Kos, which also possesses a modern airport. Rhodes is quite simply *the* Greek holiday island; Kos is smaller and quieter and has only been discovered in the last few years, so that development is on a smaller scale.

Spring in the Aegean

Rhodes is not only the larger of the two islands but also the more important from a historical and archaeological point of view, and as far as tourism is concerned. Therefore, the larger part of this book is devoted to the island of Helios. Where both islands have a similar history, this is dealt with in the first section. Events and developments peculiar to each island are described in the relevant section. Because the islands differ in many ways, it is recommended that the visitor to Rhodes also goes to Kos, and vice versa. The journey by modern hydrofoil takes only two hours.

Cherete is the Greek word for 'welcome'. Its original meaning is deeper: 'be happy'. That should not be too difficult on Rhodes and Kos.

Essential details in brief

Geographical situation: Rhodes and Kos belong to the *Dodecanese,* a group of 'twelve' islands — eighteen actually — lying off the coast of Asia Minor, from which they are separated only by a narrow stretch of sea.

Nationality: Following many changes of ownership the islands of Rhodes and Kos have belonged to Greece since May 31st 1947.

Government: Greece is a parliamentary democratic republic according to the constitution of 1975.

Language: Modern Greek. Rhodes and Kos are decidedly tourist islands, so English is generally understood. Many elderly inhabitants also speak Italian.

Religion: Greek Orthodox, with a small Muslim minority of Turkish descent.

Rhodes: The fourth largest Greek island and the main island of the Dodecanese. It has a surface area of 1412 sq. km (about the size of Gran Canaria), and is about 78 km long and up to 38 km wide. Rhodes has about 1 million tourists a year (about the same as Majorca). Rhodes town (pop. 42,000) is the capital not only of the island but of the whole Dodecanese. The total population of the island of Rhodes is about 88,000.

Kos: After Rhodes and Karpathos, Kos is the third largest of the Dodecanese islands. The capital, also named Kos, has about 12,000 inhabitants. The population of the entire island is about 21,000. The total area is 290 sq. km (half the size of Ibiza). Kos is about 50 km long and at the narrowest part barely 10 km wide. In the last few years tourism has greatly increased, and there are ample hotels of all categories.

Sources of income: Both islands are very fertile and the mild climate produces several harvests a year. Chief exports are citrus fruits, oil, vegetables and wine. Fishing is insignificant. Typical hand-made craft products include ceramics, carpets, and woven and embroidered goods. Tourism and its associated occupations are the main sources of income for both islands.

Signposts of History

4th and 3rd millennia B.C: Rhodes and Kos are colonised by a Mediterranean race, the legendary 'Pelasgians'.

2nd millennium: Phoenicians settle on Rhodes and Kos setting up bases. (The original inhabitants of Rhodes, known as 'Telchins', were probably the Phoenicians.)

About 1400: Greeks from the mainland (Achaians) establish the first fortified settlements on Rhodes.

About 1200: Trojan War.

About 1100: Dorian Greeks conquer the islands of Rhodes and Kos and turn the Achaian towns of Lindos, Ialysos and Kamiros into independent city-states.

About 800: Homer.

About 700: The three Rhodian towns together with Kos, Knidos and Halikarnassos form the Dorian League of six cities (Hexapolis). Lindos establishes its first colonies in Italy, France, Spain and North Africa.

About 550: Kleoboulos, one of the seven sages, rules over Lindos.

490/479: Persian Wars. Rhodes and Kos fight on the side of the Persians.

477: After the defeat of the Persians, Rhodes and Kos join the Delian League, the first Attic maritime confederacy.

464: Diagoras wins for Rhodes in the 79th Olympic Games. Pindar composes the seventh Olympic ode for Diagoras, in which he combines the myths and legends of Rhodes.

460: Hippocrates, the greatest doctor of ancient times, is born on Kos.

431-404: Peloponnesian War between Athens and Sparta.

411: Rhodes breaks with Athens.

408: The common capital Rhodes is founded by the three Rhodian city-states.

400/300: Rhodes temporarily comes under the influence of the Karian principality (Mausolos, Artemisia) but retains its position as a trading centre.

About 366: Founding of the capital Kos.

356: Alexander the Great is born.

334: Alexander the Great's troops occupy Rhodes. Rhodes sides with Alexander in the siege of Tyre.

333: Alexandria is founded.

323: Death of Alexander the Great. The conflict over succession leads to the Diadochian Wars (until 280 B.C.).

305/304: Demetrios Poliorketes, son of the Diadochian Antigonos, attacks Rhodes because of the island's refusal to give military aid against Ptolemaic Egypt. The siege is unsuccessful and ends in an alliance.

About 290: In memory of the siege the 'Colossus of Rhodes' is built; this is a bronze statue over 30 m high, the result of twelve years' work by the sculptor Chares of Lindos.

227: An earthquake destroys Rhodes and the Colossus of Rhodes.

3rd/2nd c: Blossoming of art and science on Rhodes.

191: Rhodes supports Rome in the war against Macedonia and Syria and is rewarded with territories in Asia Minor.

About 180–110: Panaitios of Rhodes, the famous Stoic, teaches in Rome and prepares the most aristocratic Roman families to accept Greek philosophy.

171–168: 3rd Roman-Macedonian War. Rhodes sympathises with the Macedonian King Perseus and is severely punished after Macedonia's defeat. Most of its territories in Asia Minor are confiscated; Delos is awarded the status of a free port in preference to Rhodes, thereby causing considerable damage to the latter's trade.

135–51: Poseidonios of Rhodes. This pupil of Panaitios founds a School of Rhetoric (University) where numerous noble Romans study, among them Cicero, Pompey, Caesar, Cato, Brutus, Cassius and Lucretius. Rhodes becomes prominent in the fields of art and science. The 'Laocoön Group' dates from this period.

42: Cassius, a former scholar at the University of Rhodes, lays siege to the island, conquers and plunders the town of Rhodes, and carries off 3000 statues to Rome.

A.D.51: St Paul visits Rhodes and Kos.

269: Goths conquer Rhodes.

297: The emperor Diocletian declares Rhodes a Roman province.

395: After the death of the emperor Theodosius, the Roman Empire is divided; Rhodes and Kos become part of Byzantium (Eastern Rome).

653: Arabs conquer Rhodes and sell the ruins of the Helios statue to a scrap dealer.

807: Seljuks conquer Rhodes.

1096–1099: 1st Crusade. 1099 storming of Jerusalem.

1202–1204: 4th Crusade. 1204 capture of Constantinople.

1291: Acre (Akko), the last Christian stronghold, is taken by the Mamelukes. The Crusades have failed. The Knights Templar and the Knights of St John retreat to Cyprus.

1309: The Knights of St John conquer Rhodes.

1314: The Knights of St John conquer Kos.

1453: The Turks capture Constantinople.

1479/1480: Unsuccessful siege of Rhodes by the Turks.

1522: Sultan Suleiman the Magnificent takes Rhodes and forces the Knights of St John into an honourable withdrawal from Rhodes and Kos.

1523–1912: Rhodes and Kos are under Turkish rule.

1911–1912: Italian-Turkish War. The Dodecanese are occupied by the Italians.

1943: During the Second World War, following the fall of Mussolini, there is heavy fighting between the Germans and Italians. Rhodes and Kos are under German occupation.

1945: End of Second World War. Rhodes and Kos come under British administration.

1947: Rhodes, Kos and the other Dodecanese islands are returned to Greece.

The Major Greek Gods

Zeus

Gaia (terra mater)
By herself the earth goddess produced Ouranos (Uranus), and many others.

Titans
With her son and consort Ouranos, Gaia produced the *Titans* including *Kronos, Okeanos, Iapetos, Rhea* and *Hyperion* (the father of *Helios*).

Gods
Kronos and his sister Rhea produced *Zeus* (Jupiter), *Poseidon* (Neptune), *Hades* (Pluto), *Hera* (Juno), *Hestia* (Vesta) and *Demeter* (Ceres).

The three brothers divided the world between them. Zeus received Olympos and overall power, Poseidon the sea, and Hades the underworld. With his sister and consort Hera, Zeus fathered the gods *Ares* (Mars), *Hephaistos* (Vulcan), *Hebe* and *Eileithyia*; alone he produced *Pallas Athena* (Minerva); with *Leto, Apollo* and *Artemis* (Diana), with *Maia, Hermes* (Mercury), and with *Dione, Aphrodite* (Venus).

Aphrodite

Athena

Poseidon

Hera

Heroes

As well as creating a new generation of gods through his unions with the goddesses (or nymphs), Zeus, through his countless love affairs with beautiful mortal women, also produced the half-gods (heroes), the mediators between the world of the gods and that of the humans. Some of the more important ones are as follows.

The Phoenician princess Europa, whom he carried off to Crete while disguised as a bull, bore him *Minos*, the first king of Crete; Danae, on whom he fell in the form of golden rain, produced *Perseus*; Leda, whom he approached as a swan, bore *Castor, Pollux* and *Helen*; Alkmene, whom he seduced in the guise of her husband Amphitryon, bore *Herakles* (Hercules).

Apollo

Hermes

The three windmills at Rhodes harbour

History and Legend — Rhodes
The Island of Helios

In ancient times Rhodes was called Heliusa, 'girlfriend of the sun'. According to legend, when the gods shared out the world between them they forgot Helios, the sun god, simply because he was out and about with his sun chariot. What do workers do when, having been out all day, they come home tired at night to discover they have been overlooked? They provoke a quarrel. So it was with Helios. To make things worse, he was the son of the Titan Hyperion and, like Zeus himself, one of the oldest of the nobility. He also held one of the most important positions. It was dangerous to upset him, for should he refuse to drive across the sky in his sun chariot the world would sink into eternal darkness.

Zeus offered to cancel the lottery, but the problem was solved more easily than had been supposed. For on his travels Helios had discovered an island that was still unborn.

Helios kept one thing quiet: he had seen not only an island but also a magnificent woman. This was Rhodon, a daughter of Poseidon, the god of the sea. He made the Olympians swear before the goddess of destiny that the island should belong to him. Together with the island he won the beautiful nymph Rhodon, and took her for his wife.

Rhodon means rose, but it also describes the blossom of the pomegranate, and even today scholars puzzle over whether the civic coat of arms stamped on the coins depicts a stylised rose or, more precisely, pomegranate blossom. This is a matter best left to botanists and archaeologists.

Myth is reality expressed in imagery. Geologists inform us that Rhodes was lifted up out of the sea by a submarine earthquake; as the most mysterious statue on the island was found on the sea bed, this is called 'The Venus of the Sea'.

Island of the Heliads

Helios and Rhodon had seven sons. Four of them killed one of their brothers and were banished for his murder. The other two built a town on *Mt Philerimos*. The older one, Othimos, became king and married the nymph Hegitoria, who bore him a daughter, Kydippi. Kydippi married her father's brother, thereby ensuring that the family retained power, and presented her uncle and husband Kerkaphos with three sons, Lindos, Kamiros and Ialysos. The god's grandchildren, named Heliads after him, divided up the island between them and founded the three towns which still bear their names.

This is the point where history overlaps Greek mythology in its account of the Greek occupation of Rhodes. It is now known that as early as the third millennium B.C. the island played an important role in Aegean trade, and that about 1700 B.C. the Phoenicians conquered Rhodes, established ports with organised administration and, much more importantly, were responsible for introducing to the Occident an alphabet which still forms the basis of our own. Europe, in fact, is named after a Phoenician princess, whom Zeus, in the guise of a bull, abducted and carried off to Crete.

Former Hospital of the Knights, Rhodes — now a museum

Turkey is visible 18 km from Rhodes

Rhodes is only 18 km from Asia Minor; its strategic situation between the Orient and the Occident has influenced history and is still an important factor today.

It is often said, and not without good reason, that the great culture of Crete arose from the interaction between western and eastern influences. On Rhodes, however, which seemed predestined for such interaction, this did not take place until many centuries later and with quite different results. Even in its heyday Creto-Minoan culture, which lasted more than a thousand years, remarkably did not reach Rhodes. Only when it collapsed did it have any significance for the island. In about 1450 B.C., when the great palaces and cities of Crete began to fall into decay — we still do not know exactly why — the first Minoans settled on Rhodes. Even this fact is preserved in the myth which relates that Althaimenes, a grandson of King Minos, left Crete because an oracle prophesied that he would kill his father. So he sailed for Rhodes and founded there a Cretan town, Kritinia. However, man cannot escape his destiny; Krateus sought his son, who, thinking that the old man was a robber, killed him. This is a Rhodian version of the Oedipus tragedy.

Kritinia lies at the foot of *Mt Atavyros*, the highest mountain on the island. On a clear day you can see Crete from the summit. Here there once stood a temple to Zeus, where he was worshipped in the form of a bull, and where bulls were sacrificed to him. Once, perhaps, even human sacrifices were made, as they were to the minotaur on Crete.

Myth, legend, past and present — all these merge on the island of Rhodes.

Island of the Heraklids

Another story brings us even closer to tangible historical events. Tlepolemos, son of Herakles, had in anger committed a murder in his home town of Argos, and on the advice of the Delphic oracle he left for Rhodes and founded three cities there as a penance.

The two stories only contradict each other superficially. The Helios myth is about prehistory, creation and the ordering of the earth by the gods, without whose power nothing can happen. On the other hand, the story of Herakles (Hercules), the son of Zeus and Alkmene, is concerned with those beings who mediate between the world of gods and that of humans. Each generation of gods stands for a new age, and each new age has its own literary form — for the gods the myth, for the heroes the saga. This dual origin was not a problem for the Rhodians, because it simply added one honour to another, and a Greek cannot have too much fame. Tlepolemos is supposed to have come to Rhodes shortly before the Trojan War, about 1200 B.C. Today it is assumed that the Achaians settled on Rhodes up to two centuries earlier and finally took over the island by continual immigration. This, in turn, occurred as the result of virtual civil war in Hellas. New Greek races had invaded Greece from the north, overthrowing the old regime and subjugating the earlier oppressors. Mycenaean culture declined in a sea of blood and tears amid the Doric invasion.

Greece sank into chaos. Yet those Achaians who had survived and wanted to remain free men absconded from the murderers. Thus began the first Greek colonisation which, in Asia Minor and the offshore islands, finally led to the birth of what is known as western culture, by the integration of western and eastern elements. Homer's epic of the Trojan War is the symbolic representation of this process. The Greeks were and are jealous admirers of beauty, so the struggle for supremacy in the Aegean was portrayed as a contest for the possession of the desirable Helen.

Homer writes that Tlepolemos supported the Greeks against Troy with a fleet of

Part of a fallen column at the Acropolis, Rhodes

Lindos

nine ships. From the Greek-Phoenician union a nation of daring seafarers went forth to trade with the whole known world. When the Dorians followed the Achaians in about 1000 B.C., they took over this tradition. 'Ten Rhodians, ten ships' soon became a familiar quotation.

Rhodians founded colonies on the coasts of Asia Minor, and in Spain, Italy and France; for example, Naukratis on the Nile Delta, Gela in Sicily, and Naples. Possibly the Rhône owes its name to them. Lindos, which had the only good natural harbour on the island, soon achieved prominence. At a time when maritime trading was almost synonymous with piracy — Homer did not regard this as a crime at all but as a totally acceptable occupation – the Lindians had already codified special maritime laws. This 'Lindian Maritime Code', the oldest known to man, still exists today. The Romans adopted this code, which they called the Lex Rhodia, and through the Byzantines it found its way into western legislation. Seafaring brought prosperity to the islands. The Rhodians, grandsons of Helios, considered it quite natural that the gods had rewarded their endeavours.

The three city-states behaved in a typically Greek manner, remaining independent and competing with one another. Lindos was the most important. About 550 B.C. Kleoboulos, one of the seven sages of the ancient world, declared himself a tyrant, an absolute ruler. A sage who is a tyrant? The unfavourable meaning of 'tyrant' comes from a later period, but at the time of Kleoboulos it simply referred to a form of government. Kleoboulos was a friend of the famous legislator, Solon of Athens, who was also an absolute ruler and sage. In fact, significant cultural achievements are linked to the names of some tyrants: Peisistratos (Athens), Polycrates (Samos), Gelon (Sicily); even Pericles belongs to this list.

On one of the capes which frame the harbour of Lindos stands a monumental round building, which tourist guides like to call the 'Grave of Kleoboulos'. The name is not correct (probably a rich shipowner was buried there about 100 B.C.), but it shows the influence which Kleoboulos had in Lindos. 'Nothing in excess' is one of the sayings attributed to him. The Greeks are very proud of this expression but have never quite taken it to heart.

Rhodes and the Colossus of Rhodes

The Rhodians, daring sailors and clear-headed mathematicians, could not survive on their own against Greece in the west or Asia Minor in the east, so they calculated the risk and opted for the side that would most probably win. They pursued a 'pendulum' policy which they adapted as circumstances changed. One has only to consult the map to see that they had no other choice.

During the Persian Wars they sided with the Persians. They were not the only ones, incidentally. History books may state that *the* Greeks fought against *the* Persians, but at times more Greeks fought on the Persian side than on the Greek side. Following the Persian defeat, Rhodes joined the Delian League, but only flourished itself when the power of Athens diminished and finally collapsed in the Peloponnesian War (431–404 B.C.). In 411 the Rhodians broke with Athens and, at the same time, decided that the age of the small city-states was over. They changed course and resolved to build a single capital on the north-eastern tip of the island. This revolutionary decision not only led to the self-sacrifice of the three glorious cities, but more importantly it brought about a decisive break with tradition. About fifty years later Kos took the same step.

Greek culture of the Classical period is a *polis* culture, a small-town culture. The excessive particularism which, until the last century, prevented Greek national unity is both cause and effect of the theory that one could only lead a worthy life in the polis, that is, in the ordered small town. The Greeks found the cities of Asia Minor to be barbaric and frightening, and when the polis could no longer accommodate the growing population they preferred to found another town rather than over-extend the original polis.

The outline of the town was true to the plan: a rational system of straight roads, intersecting at right angles, which ran north-south and east-west creating a chessboard pattern. This principle, named after its inventor Hippodamos of Miletus, became the rule for most Hellenistic cities and was indeed the basic pattern of innumerable towns, right up to modern times. Not until motorised traffic arrived did the street pattern radically alter. The street patterns of Rhodes are still clearly recognisable, but regrettably little remains of the ancient town.

The writers of antiquity were united in their admiration of Rhodes. For example, the geographer Strabo wrote: 'The town of Rhodes lies on the eastern tip of the island and stands out from others by its harbours, its streets and walls, and its general layout, so that we cannot name any other town that is similar, let alone superior. The quality and justice of the state constitution and the diligence of the government in all matters, particularly in maritime affairs, are impressive, which is why the city ruled the seas for so long and was able to destroy the scourge of piracy and establish friendships with the Romans and with the kings who were allies of Rome and Greece. So it remained independent and was embellished with various treasures, most of which are to be found in the Temple of Dionysus and in the Gymnasium, though there are others elsewhere. A quite magnificent example is the huge statue of the sun god with an iambic inscription: "Chares of Lindos built me, seventy yards tall". Today the Colossus lies on the ground, brought down by an earthquake to knee height. In accordance with an oracle it was never rebuilt.'

The Colossus of Rhodes was one of the Seven Wonders of the World and its early history was most remarkable.

The Colossus of Rhodes

It took Rhodes exactly 100 years to take advantage of the changing political circumstances through skilful manoeuvring. Even Alexander the Great was unable to force Rhodes to its knees by founding the rival port of Alexandria. (Incidentally, Alexander's most capable opponent in the Persian campaigns was the Rhodian Memnon.) Yet after Alexander's death (323 B.C.), when his generals were fighting over the division of his huge empire, Rhodes too became involved in the maelstrom of the Diadochian Wars.

The one-eyed Antigonos succeeded, after eventful struggles, in uniting a considerable part of the empire under his control. His best general was his own son Demetrios, who had the frightening nickname Poliorketes, 'destroyer of towns'. After father and son had gained a glorious victory over the Ptolemaic fleet at Salamis in 306 they wanted to conquer Egypt as well and demanded the support of Rhodes.

The Rhodians, always inclined towards neutrality, refused; they had to refuse, because for them trade with Alexandria and the Ptolemaic empire was crucial. Antigonos was not prepared to accept this revolt and sent his son to bring Rhodes to its senses.

In 305 Demetrios appeared with a fleet of 400 ships and about 50,000 men. At this time Rhodes itself had about 6,000 citizens capable of defending the town. Despite this the situation was not desperate. Egypt and Crete sent auxiliary forces and the slaves were promised their freedom if they fought bravely. So the Rhodians were able to oppose Demetrios with some 25,000 soldiers.

The powerful bastions were not easy to take and they hoped that their fleet would be able to prevent a blockade, so although they did not regard the prospect of a siege with total complacency it was not felt necessary to surrender. On the other hand Demetrios had brought with him fearsome siege weapons, partly of his own invention, some of which were assembled in advance on his huge ships. He was determined to force the issue.

Despite tremendous efforts he did not succeed in taking the harbour, which he needed to supply his forces. The weather came to the aid of the Rhodians; storms caused severe damage among Demetrios' ships and the Rhodian fleet kept the sea lanes free.

Then Demetrios changed his tactics; he had a unique siege machine built which was of fantastic dimensions — the *helepolis*. It was a 50-m-high and 25-m-wide square tower on wheels. Its nine storeys contained a myriad of catapults, battering rams and scaling ladders; it towered above the town walls, and so Demetrios was justifiably confident. Almost three and a half thousand men were necessary to set the giant tower in motion. Then it rolled terrifyingly towards the walls and immediately smashed a wide gap in them. Still the Rhodians did not capitulate, but carried on fighting until nightfall. The helepolis was armoured from top to bottom with animal skins and wickerwork, but was so badly damaged that Demetrios, fuming with rage, had to give the order to withdraw and repair it. The Rhodians had won a breathing space, but the decisive onslaught was still to come. At the second attempt the attackers actually did penetrate the city, and even the Rhodians' furious defence could not have postponed their fate any longer if the cunning civil engineer Diognetos had not directed the town's sewers into the path of the helepolis. The destroyer of cities sank ridiculously into the filth, at the same time blocking the path of the main forces. This bloody tragi-comedy was ended through a *deus ex machina*, that is by Antigonos himself, who wrote to his son to say he should return as quickly as possible, because he needed him and his army elsewhere.

It could not have worked out better for either side. On the one hand Demetrios had so far failed in his conquest, and on the other the Rhodians did not know how long they could survive renewed attacks. Both kept face and made an alliance against the enemies of Antigonos, excluding the Ptolemaic forces. The unvanquished congratulated themselves and retained their self-esteem, and Demetrios handed over all his armaments to the Rhodians. They decided to sell them and, with the proceeds, erect a gigantic statue of the sun god, the island's protector, in commemoration of the siege. The sale brought in 300 talents, about half a million pounds.

It is assumed that the commission was given to the sculptor Chares of Lindos, of whom little is known, other than that he was supposed to have been a pupil of the great Lysippos. There is a charming story that Chares was first asked to present a model and estimate for an average-sized statue, and was then requested to produce a statue twice the size for double the price.

Chares is said to have spent twelve years working on the Colossus which was therefore finished about 290 B.C., but it collapsed in a devastating earthquake in 227 B.C.

The source of the funding, the approximate date of origin and the size of the statue (a good 30 m) are all known. What is not known is how it was possible to make a bronze statue of such dimensions, where it stood, what it looked like, and the real reason why it was never re-erected.

Technically, at any rate, it was a masterpiece. It is assumed that it consisted of 'small' individual pieces which were later soldered together, and that the statue was set upright by stacking massive piles of earth. The interior was hollow, and perhaps it was even possible to walk inside it; its head was said to have had the capacity of 22 cartloads of wheat. The statue was reinforced inside by iron pegs, and stabilised by heavy pieces of rock.

The inscription reads:
'To the peak of Olympos, oh Helios, the Doric people of Rhodes built this Colossus of bronze in your praise, as they finally appease the waves of violent war and adorn their homeland with splendid booty. They built it firmly on the earth and high over the sea so that it should be for them a magnificent beacon of unrestricted freedom. It is the right of the men of the blood of Herakles to rule the land and sea as their fathers have done.'

The assumption that the Colossus stood astride the harbour entrance originated in the Baroque imagination of Fischer von Erlach. Everything contradicts this theory — technically, archaeologically and psychologically. The statistical problems would have multiplied; the ruins would have blocked the harbour entrance, yet there is no evidence of this and not a trace of the statue has been found. Finally it is highly improbable that a consecrated gift would have been profaned as a lighthouse (although the Statue of Liberty in New York was conceived in accordance with this lighthouse theory). The most probable site was in front of the Temple of Helios, but even this supposition will remain unresolved. After the great earthquake destroyed both the statue and the city, a worldwide appeal for Rhodes began. The town arose

Courtyard of the Grand Master's Palace, Rhodes

like a phoenix from the ashes, but the statue was not rebuilt because Delphi advised against it. There were ugly rumours that the Rhodians had made use of the oracle because they wanted the money for a different purpose. A more sympathetic, and probably more correct, opinion is that the earthquake was interpreted as a sign from the gods, whom they did not want to anger again with their arrogance. The ruins amazed following generations. Pliny wrote: 'There are only a few people who can grasp his thumb; even the fingers are larger than most entire statues. There are gaping holes in the broken off limbs.'

So the fragments of the sun god lay for nine hundred years, until they were sold by the Arabian General Muawija in A.D.653 to a scrap dealer, who carted them away on 'nine hundred' camels, which is no doubt merely an eastern way of saying 'very many'.

Island of Artists

There is practically no other single work of art which has had a more lasting influence on European intellectual thought than has the *Laocoön group*. It was discovered in Rome in 1506 — at exactly the right time. Its discovery created a tremendous sensation, and for the Renaissance it had the effect of a spark in a powder keg. This was reality, something Michelangelo was still only dreaming about — the human body represented in extreme excitement, and at the same time restrained by the magic of form.

This masterpiece of western art, created in the first century B.C. by Hagesandros, Polydoros and Athanodoros, originated in Rhodes, and this was no accident. One of the chief attractions of the Louvre is the *Victory of Samothrace*,

Serpents sent by Apollo attack Laocoön and his sons (Vatican Museum)

which is also a Rhodian creation, as is the *Farnese Bull* in the Museum of Naples.

When Cassius plundered Rhodes in A.D. 42, he carried off to Rome no fewer than three thousand statues, probably the biggest art theft in history. Then he set fire to the town. Politically Rhodes never really recovered from this destruction; yet 1500 years later a single work of art from the Rhodian school of sculpture, the Laocoön group in fact, achieved a considerable and lasting victory — the triumph of spirit over might. The Rhodians had learnt seafaring from the Phoenicians, and their artistic skill from the Minoans. The astonishing birth of Athene from the head of Zeus was supposed to have taken place in Lindos, and the name of the goddess who protects artists suggests Cretan origins. The descendants kept both traditions alive, and their interaction gives Rhodian art its special character. The ships not only transported goods all over the world, they also brought back ideas from every land. From the very beginning Rhodian art was subject to international and cosmopolitan influences; it picked up foreign stimuli, assimilated them and developed them further. The Museum of Rhodes houses a wealth of examples of the successful blending of western and eastern elements.

The craftsmanship of Rhodian bronze sculpture is undoubtedly demonstrated by the statue of Helios. The respect it commanded in society at large is illustrated by an anecdote concerning the aforementioned siege, of which the Colossus was the only significant legacy. While Demetrios' troops were furiously storming the city walls and were only being driven back with great difficulty by the Rhodians, Protegenes sat in his house outside the city walls, painting a picture of Ialysos as a hunter. He had been working for seven years on the painting and did not allow the siege to distract him. The Rhodians were worried for his safety and that of his work, and they sent a delegation to Demetrios, asking him to guarantee Protegenes' safety. Demetrios sent for Protegenes and asked him how he managed to carry on painting so calmly in such a situation. The pair were a match for each other. 'I know that you wage wars against nations but not against artists,' said Protegenes; Demetrios replied, 'I'd rather burn my own father's paintings than destroy such a work of art,' and he provided Protegenes with a bodyguard.

During the last two centuries B.C. the Rhodian school of sculpture flourished. The Rhodian style, predestined by its international character for the cosmopolitan Hellenistic era, led the way; it is calculated that at this time more than a dozen studios were working in close proximity to each other. It is often maintained that cultural brilliance is connected with political power, and as examples people like to cite Rome under Augustus, England under Elizabeth, and France under Louis XIV. Rhodes is one of the principal exceptions.

The extraordinary respect that Rhodes enjoyed in the ancient world is illustrated by the widespread sympathy and help it received after the earthquake in 227 B.C. However, it was not until the next century, when the island was no longer able to maintain its policy of neutrality and became a satellite of Rome, that it achieved world status in the arts. The victors adopted the culture of the vanquished; Greek philosophers taught the sons of the Roman aristocracy and thus became the teachers of Europe. One of the most important thinkers of this time, who originated from Lindos but taught in Rome, is the Stoic Panaitios (190–110 B.C.), a friend of the younger Scipio, the victor of Carthage. His pupil Poseidonios (135–51 B.C.) founded a sort of university in Rhodes, the fame of which was so legendary that for the best Roman families it became a mark of taste to send their sons there.

The significance that this school had for Europe is shown by a few names: Cicero, who studied rhetoric here; Caesar, who fell into the hands of pirates on the journey and had to be ransomed at a high price; his friend and murderer Brutus; Pompey, of whom it is said that he presented each philosopher with the gift of one talent, a very high sum; the poet Lucretius; and the emperor Tiberius. However, Cassius proved that educating the intellect is not enough. He forgot all his youthful memories of Rhodes and, disregarding the wise counsel of his teacher, Archelaos, captured, plundered and destroyed the island.

On the Acropolis of Rhodes there is a restored amphitheatre with 800 seats, but no stage. It was not an actual theatre but an odeion, an open-air auditorium.

Close by is the stadium. Education always meant both physical and intellectual training. The saying *mens sana in corpore sano* (a healthy mind in a healthy body) was adopted by the Romans from the Greeks.

Almost everything that Is known about the myths and legends of Rhodes comes from a victory ode for a sportsman, Diagoras from Ialysos, who won the boxing for Rhodes in the 79th Olympic Games. Pindar, the greatest poet of the time, honoured the greatest athlete of the time with a song. In the 5th c. B.C. the Olympic Games were more a religious than a sporting occasion. Whoever won the olive branch was awarded the highest honour a mortal could receive. Zeus himself had conferred victory upon him! Diagoras had won not only in Olympia but in several national Greek competitions. As if that were not enough, his sons also became Olympic victors. When they carried their father through the stadium the people went wild.

Diagoras died soon afterwards, and he will have heard with satisfaction on the other side that even his grandsons continued the family tradition.

Below: Entrance to Mandraki Harbour, Rhodes. Right: Acropolis, Lindos.

Philerimos

Island of Knights

The Order of the Knights of St John dates from the time of the Crusades. In 1070 citizens of the town of Amalfi founded, with the consent of the Egyptian authorities, a hospital in Jerusalem for the care of sick pilgrims. The institute took the name of the holy patriarch, John the Compassionate. Its members took the monastic vows and joined the Benedictine order.

They lived harmoniously together until the Crusaders appeared. Then the town commander banned the brethren from Jerusalem, and they thereupon joined the conquering army. The master of the order at that time, Gerhard, seems to have given the knights good advice, for the brotherhood was provided with generous funds by the Franks and awarded independent status by Pope Paschalis II in 1113. The order took the name of 'Knights Hospitaller' and was directly subordinate to the Holy See. About the same time the Order of the Knights Templar was founded. The Hospitallers, who in accordance with the warlike atmosphere of the time assumed the objectives of the Templars, discovered that it was not enough merely to care for the sick, but that they also had to protect the pilgrims, something which had not been necessary before the Crusades.

At the end of the Crusades in 1270 the Knights Templar and Hospitallers withdrew to Cyprus, where they were rather begrudgingly offered asylum and did not know what they should do. Their legendary wealth had long excited widespread envy and had to be legitimised by military successes. Actually a new Crusade was agreed between Pope Clement and Philip IV of France, but it soon became clear that it was aimed less at the Holy Land than at the wealth of the Knights Templar. In 1307 Philip had all the Templars in his jurisdiction arrested and charged with treason. The Pope commanded the remaining princes to follow his example. Bribed witnesses and torture did their business; the order was banned, its property confiscated and the Grand Master burnt at the stake in Paris in 1314.

At that time Rhodes was theoretically still part of the Byzantine Empire but in practice it was the pirates who ruled. With the consent of the Genoese Vignolo de Vignoli they carried out raids against Arabs, Turks, Venetians and anybody else who came into sight in the eastern Aegean. Vignoli had leased the islands of Kos and Leros from the Byzantine Emperor Andronikos, but saw his activities increasingly limited by the Turks on one side and the Knights of St John operating from Cyprus on the other. Why attack each other, Vignoli asked, and presented the Grand Master of the Knights of St John, Fulk de Villaret, with an ingenious plan: jointly to conquer Rhodes and the Dodecanese and share the booty. Vignoli would be satisfied with a third.

The strategic importance of the island of Rhodes, which is like a spear aimed at Asia Minor, was apparent. Rhodes was also orientated towards Constantinople, the eternal goal of western expansion. Vignoli saw the occupation of Rhodes as an insignificant detail. While he was making preparations, Fulk sailed to Europe to seek Papal consent. Of course, it was granted. Even the Pope was able to kill two birds with one stone. On the one hand Rhodes was an ideal base for attacking the east (whether one regarded the Muslims or the Orthodox Christians as opponents), and on the other the quarrelsome knights were meaningfully occupied and so were not causing any trouble for him. With the highest level of approval they set off. The fleet first anchored off Feraklos and, while Vignoli tried in vain to take Rhodes, Fulk sent a deputation to the emperor requesting him to hand over the island. In return for this the knights offered to rid the island and surrounding seas of pirates and install 300 knights as loyal servants.

But Andronikos had not forgotten the pillage of Constantinople of a hundred years before, and refused. The knights, outraged at the insult, launched a major attack. The first goal was *Philerimos*, the dominating mountain castle to the south of the city. Treachery gained this for them; a servant, taking revenge for a beating he had received, led the knights to an unguarded door.

For a long time that was the only victory. Vignoli had thought conquest would be a trifling matter, but it proved to be a time-consuming exercise. Only at the end of a two-year siege did the city capitulate. On August 15th 1309 the Knights of St John moved into Rhodes. In the west the victory of western Christianity over the east was viewed as a great triumph. The Knights of St John now called themselves 'Chevaliers de Rhodes'. Nowadays this is the name of a good red wine.

The knights settled down and built — or rather made their Greek subjects build — a gigantic fortress, which still amazes the visitor today. Within the walls stand the Grand Master's Palace, a fortress in itself, and the knights' quarter *Collachium*, which was in turn separated from the Greek town by its own wall. The Street of the Knights has been carefully restored, and today is a fine example of pure late Gothic. Each of the nations, or 'Tongues', had its own hostel here, each subordinate to its own prior: France, Auvergne, Provence, Aragon, Castile, Germany, England and Italy. The French had the upper hand as the division into three languages gave them an important advantage, for votes were distributed according to tongues rather than according to the number of knights. For this reason the Spanish sub-divided into Castile and Aragon at the earliest opportunity.

The order had not completely forgotten its original purpose. The hospital, now a museum, was strictly run in an exemplary fashion; the doctors, for example, had instructions to make their rounds twice a day. The small chambers in the main hall were used as sleeping quarters for the pilgrims.

The real reason for the presence here of the Knights of St John lay elsewhere. Rhodes was now the most easterly outpost of the west, and as the struggles against the Muslims on land had been lost the knights took it up again at sea. They had to protect Christian ships against the Turkish pirates — a task which they undertook with great devotion, especially as it made it easy to legitimise their own piracy. Even Vignoli was able to harvest the 'fruits of the sea' with a clear conscience. As early as Homer's time, it was difficult to separate seafaring from piracy, and now it was really no longer possible to distinguish what Christian duty ordered or at least permitted. In the war against the infidels there were no rules. Certainly, if the knights, as rumour had it, occasionally disguised themselves and their crew as Turks in order to capture Venetian ships, then religious duty had overstepped the mark. Whatever the truth, law, order and discipline prevailed on Rhodes itself, and not only did the order become rich but so did the island itself. The knights took three vows: poverty, chastity and obedience. The first one related only to the individual. The order itself was anything but poor, and after the Knights of St John had acquired the possessions of their unfortunate competitors, the Templars, they were thought to be richer than all the rest of the Church put together. In the long run this had an effect on the personal lifestyle of the knights. The second vow was essentially defined as celibacy; but the third vow of obedience was rigidly observed. Even if the different national groups quarrelled among themselves, they nevertheless outwardly presented a united front. The Collachium was closely guarded; the knights were only allowed to leave it on horseback or in pairs, a practice which did not exactly make for a close understanding with the population. In the soft air of Rhodes the gentlemen 'with the iron fists and unconquerable hearts' must have been a surprising sight. 'They omitted to live in the spirit of Christ, yet they were prepared to die for it.' Nothing illustrates the accuracy of this statement by Gibbons more clearly than the history of the sieges of Rhodes.

In 1479, 25 years after the capture of Constantinople, the Turks appeared for the first time off the island. They were driven back. But the following year Sultan Mehmed II, the conqueror of Constantinople, landed 70,000 men in a fleet of 160 ships. After a three-month attack he succeeded in breaking through. The knights fought like lions. They were only saved by the ineptitude of the Turkish commander who, whether for humanitarian or egotistical reasons, refused his men permission to pillage. His soldiers did not want to risk their lives for honour alone; the attack came to a standstill. Grand Master Pierre d'Aubusson exploited the temporary

Entrance to the Grand Master's Palace, Rhodes

indecision with an audacious attack, captured the standard and drove the Turks to flight. 9000 Turks met with an ignominious death. The 8000 posts which had been rammed in to impale the besieged became instead a defensive palisade. Almost half of the knights were killed.

The survivors immediately began to strengthen the walls, for it was obvious that the Ottoman rulers would not take this defeat lying down. They worked feverishly: the ramparts were widened to twelve metres; new moats were dug; new bastions appeared. Rhodes became the strongest fortress in the west. The uneasy peace lasted 42 years. Then Sultan Suleiman the Magnificent, the conqueror of Belgrade, began the assault. 'This island has been a thorn in my side for too long,' he said.

He made extensive preparations for war and demanded that the Knights of St John surrender, because 'where my army treads everyone dies by the terrible blades of our swords'. The almost seventy-year-old Grand Master, Villiers de l'Isle Adam, refused. Suleiman was not a man of half measures. He equipped a fleet of 600 ships, manned by 40,000 oarsmen, which transported to Rhodes the actual troops — 25,000 heavily armed soldiers, supported by 60,000 engineers. In the castle were 600 knights, 400 Cretans and 6,000 Greeks. A comparison with the siege by Demetrios comes to mind, in that both sides proved not only their bravery but also their respect for each other.

Naturally, the Turks first occupied the offshore islands and Mt Philerimos before launching the real attack. After six months' bitter fighting the knights had to concede that their situation was hopeless. Betrayal accelerated the surrender but was not decisive. The age of the knights had passed.

Even while the ceasefire negotiations were still continuing at Christmas 1522, the Turks surged into the city and caused a terrible bloodbath among the Greek population. It was horrific. However, one must remember Jerusalem and Constantinople, and the massacres which took place in 1365 when the Crusaders captured Alexandria.

Suleiman tried nevertheless to put a stop to the destruction as soon as possible, and on January 1st 1523 the 180 knights who had survived left the island, together with 4,000 Catholic Rhodians who were also granted safe passage. The knights went first to Cyprus, from where they had sailed 215 years before, but they had to wait another nine years until they were allotted Malta as a real home. Thus the Knights of St John became the Maltese.

'They have sown the wind, and they shall reap the storm,' said Suleiman before the attack.

'Nothing in the world was lost so gloriously as Rhodes,' said Charles V after the surrender. It is all a matter of perspective.

Island of the Turks and Italians

Considering the Turks were in control of Rhodes for almost 400 years, they left remarkably few traces behind. When you sail into the harbour you are immediately struck by the sight of the many minarets, a scene which has been described a thousand times. The silhouette of Rhodes shows at a glance the entire complicated history of the island. There are the powerful bastions of the knights, the Grand Master's Palace, the Turkish minarets, the Byzantine cupolas, the Catholic campaniles, the Italian new town, the modern hotels. It is ancient Rhodes that is

*Map of Rhodes
in 1480 depicting
the Turkish
army besieging
the knights
(Bibliothèque
Nationale)*

missing; you have to look hard to find that. It is a complicated business and you
need to take your time observing and reflecting on the scene. At first sight you will
probably overestimate the influence of the Turks. Nine out of ten mosques used to
be Byzantine churches (and some have become so again); minarets have merely
been added.

The number of Turks who lived on Rhodes was never very large. Today there are
still about 2000 Muslims, who worship only in the Suleiman Mosque. Even this is a
reconstruction, like so much on Rhodes. In its present form it dates from 1808.

Quite genuine on the other hand is the Murad Reis Mosque, named after the
Egyptian admiral who was significantly involved in the conquest of Rhodes and who
lies buried in the mosque. The walk through the picturesque graveyard is not to be
missed.

To say that the Turks were better conquerors than administrators contradicts the
usual western idea. However, not only is Rhodes proof of this, but so are Greece
and the whole of the Balkans. The relatively small upper classes were interested
neither in fighting nor in religion. The pashas wanted as many taxes, as little trouble
and as pleasant a life as possible. All it meant to the local people was a change of

foreign overlord, both in the town and in the castles.

During the Turkish period Rhodes was overcome more by lethargy than terror. Apart from the mosques very little remains from the Ottoman era. Exceptions are the interesting library opposite the Suleiman Mosque, which houses the most valuable Arab manuscripts (which, however, even the Turks can no longer read); the splendid Turkish bath, destroyed in the war but rebuilt and still in use; the picturesque Turkish quarter, now inhabited almost entirely by Greeks; the busy oriental bazaar concentrated around Socrates Street; and a few lovely houses, with typical balconies and window grilles, for the women of the harem.

In the course of time things settled down. The Greeks were granted a kind of self-government, and the houses of the rich shipowners at Lindos bear witness to the fact that by no means all Greek activity was stifled. The Greek revolt of 1821 led to a crisis. Indeed, after a heroic ten-year struggle it resulted in the liberation of mainland Greece. However, the population of Rhodes, naturally sympathetic towards their motherland, had to suffer Turkish reprisals, and in spite of all the sacrifices the great powers (England, France and Russia) thought it right to leave the Dodecanese Islands to the Ottoman Empire.

Not until 1912 did the hour of liberation arrive. The Italian-Turkish war led to the occupation of the islands by the Italians, who were greeted as friends by the Greeks and immediately proclaimed that they did not intend to stay. Perhaps this was their genuine intention at the time. However, the Italians found increasing pleasure in the islands, and during the era of Fascism the Greeks suffered a great deal under the Italian occupation.

Under Mussolini Rhodes became a cornerstone of the new 'Imperium Romanum'. The reconstruction of the Grand Master's Palace, which had been destroyed by an explosion in 1856, is a demonstration of this political ambition. The Italians have had to endure much abuse because of this. The palace, especially its interior, is obviously an example of Fascist megalomania, and it is only worth visiting for its marvellous views, and for the beautiful Hellenistic mosaics which were brought here from Kos.

The Greeks had numerous problems to face. Italian became a compulsory subject in schools, and as far as possible Greek was suppressed. The Italians tried to drive out the Greeks and settle as many of their compatriots as they could, and it is understandable if the Rhodians still speak badly of them. Nevertheless, all this does not alter the fact that modern-day Rhodes owes a great deal to the Italians.

The Italians laid out the modern new town — surprisingly in Arab style – as a well tended garden town with many parks. They set in motion a programme of afforestation on Rhodes and Kos, chiefly using experts from the Alto Adige; they painstakingly restored the antiquities (even if, seen from today's standpoint, this was sometimes overdone); they created an excellent road network which facilitates travel by car between nearly all the important places on the island; they laid out model agricultural villages which still exist, separately from but alongside the Greek settlements. In short, they have decidedly improved the infrastructure of the island. The fact that they did not necessarily do this to benefit the Greeks is immaterial.

In 1943, when Italy broke with Germany, there was heavy fighting between the former allies, particularly on Mt Philerimos. Today the traces of this conflict have almost completely disappeared. Rhodes was occupied first by the Germans, then by the British who ruled as trustees for the United Nations. In 1947 the Dodecanese Islands were finally returned to Greece. Rhodes only recovered slowly

Rhodes old town leading to the Sultan Suleiman Mosque

from the destruction of the war. A decisive change was brought about by mass tourism, which today is the principal means of livelihood for the islanders.

The Press Officer of the British Military Administration was Lawrence Durrell. During his two-year stay he wrote a most charming book about Rhodes, 'Reflections on a Marine Venus'.

Durrell's memories are more than a delightful account of his experiences – they are a uniquely enchanting declaration of his affection for the island. Once again defenceless Rhodes had captivated a conqueror through its scenery, its climate, its history and its beauty. On his departure Durrell wrote: 'Ahead of us the night gathers, a different night, and Rhodes begins to fall into the unresponding sea from which only memory can rescue it. The clouds hang high over Anatolia. Other islands? Other futures? Not, I think, after one has lived with the Marine Venus. The wound she gives one must carry to the world's end.'

History of Kos

Evidence of the first settlement can be traced to the 4th millennium B.C. The original inhabitants, who are said to have belonged to the legendary race of Pelasgians, were followed in the 2nd millennium by Karians from Asia Minor (which is why the island was first called Kouris or Karis) who ploughed the fertile plains. About 1600 B.C. the Cretan Minoans founded a trading colony on the site of the present capital. With the collapse of the Minoan empire in the 15th c. B.C. the Achaians and then the Mycenaeans followed in waves; there is also evidence of Phoenician strongholds. Together with Karpathos, Nisyros, Kassos and Kalymnos the Koans took part in the Trojan War (about 1200 B.C.) with thirty ships, an indication of considerable wealth.

The Mycenaean empires were overrun and destroyed by the Dorian Greeks, and thus begins the 'dark age' of Greek history about which little is known. According to Herodotos, Dorians from Epidauros settled on Kos in the 9th c. B.C. (a fact which is confirmed by discoveries of ceramics), and probably about this period brought to the island the Asklepios cult, which later made Kos famous and rich. About 700 B.C. Kos joined with the three Rhodian towns of Lindos, Ialysos and Kamiros together with Knidos and Halikarnassos in Asia Minor to form the Doric 'League of Six Cities' (Hexapolis), a union with political and religious aims.

There was no question of central administration. Following the old Greek tradition, the regions led their own separate lives. The most important town was Astypalaia (in the bay of Kefalos in the south-west), whose unfavourable location from the point of view of trade proves again that the Koans were not concerned with the sea but with their own fertile land.

Following the Persian victory over the Lydians in 546 B.C., Kos, together with the coast of Asia Minor and the neighbouring islands, was subject to Persian domination and, equipped with five ships, had to participate on the side of the Persians in the battle of Salamis. Not until after the final Persian defeat by the Greeks (479 B.C.) did Kos become independent to some extent, and in 477 it joined the Delian League under the dominance of Athens. The contribution which Kos made to the alliance is evidence that the island was able to maintain its prosperity despite all these vicissitudes.

During Greece's Classical era, the 5th and 4th centuries B.C., Kos flourished, particularly as the island succeeded in keeping out of the internal civil war between Athens and Sparta (Peloponnesian War 431–404) for most of the time. However, there is practically nothing to see on Kos of this very complicated period of history. Historians and archaeologists have painstakingly reconstructed it from scripts and fragments. The defeat of Athens by Sparta was likewise useful to Kos since Athens had increasingly exploited its position of superiority in the alliance. However, Kos was not completely unaffected by the internal conflicts within Greece after the end of the war. The formation of a pro-Attic (democratic) party and a pro-Spartan party (an oligarchy) almost led to civil war. This was ended by a compromise which was to be of exceptional significance for Kos: following the example of Rhodes (see page 15) both parties decided to build a joint capital on the north-eastern tip of the island — where it still stands today. This decision was facilitated by the destruction of Astypalaia by a devastating earthquake around 412 B.C., when some of its population fled to Cape Skandari.

After Alexander the Great and the disagreements over his successor (Diadochian Wars) Kos came under Ptolemaic (Egyptian) rule, and from 130 B.C. like the rest of Greece under Roman rule. As the Romans (and all the other conquerors) valued Kos greatly and the reputation of the sanctuary of Asklepios had spread throughout the entire Ancient World, the Hellenistic centuries brought remarkable prosperity to Kos. Most of the impressive archaeological exhibits date from this period.

The apostle Paul visited Kos on his travels and laid the foundations for Christianity which — as the ruins of many early Christian churches suggest — spread relatively quickly. After the division of the Roman Empire (A.D. 395) Kos became part of Byzantium and came under the jurisdiction of the administrative region of Samos. After the fourth Crusade in 1204 Kos became a Venetian duchy (under the name Lango) and a century later went over to Genoa, whose representative Vignolo de Vignoli signed the famous treaty with the Order of the Knights of St John which eventually brought both Rhodes and Kos under the domination of the Knights. Kos became an outpost of Rhodes and the two islands fell to the Turks in 1523.

Turkish rule lasted almost 400 years until Italian troops occupied the Dodecanese islands in the Italian-Turkish war of 1911–12, and rapidly settled there, contrary to the original proclamations.

Particularly during the Fascist era, the Greeks had to suffer the difficulties imposed by the Italian administration. Following the break between Germany and Italy in 1943 Kos was occupied by German troops and towards the end of the war by British troops. In 1947 all the Dodecanese islands were returned to Greece.

Food and Drink

You could describe Greek cooking as being somewhere between the cuisine of Italy and that of the Middle East. Greek cuisine is characterised by the use of oil, olives, tomatoes, artichokes, peppers, garlic, onions, lamb and mutton, sheep's and goat's cheese, and grapes. These are the main ingredients. On the coast there are, of course, fish and seafood of every kind. All this is accompanied by an aniseed spirit (*ouzo*) and resinated wine (*retsina*).

Most visitors like to sample the specialities of the country which they are visiting. However, in all the tourist areas the hotels have been catering for foreign visitors for a long time, and regrettably this has led to uniformity in the menus.

'The fool visits the museums, the wise man the tavernas.' This saying is attributed not to a glutton or an alcoholic but to a cultivated Graecophile. So do visit the tavernas and do not be put off either by the strange language or by what seem at first to be strange tastes.

There are no communication difficulties, even if you cannot decipher the handwritten Greek menu. In larger towns and in tourist resorts the menu is usually written in several languages. If you are in any difficulty you may be invited into the kitchen where you will find displayed all the ready-cooked dishes and you can make your choice. This is not at all unusual but is customary among Greeks.

There is obviously a variety of places to eat. In the towns and main tourist centres most dishes are available, and the hotels serve international cuisine. Yet close by there are usually traditional Greek tavernas which are less expensive. This is one reason for booking half-board accommodation if possible. However, don't expect to find an elaborate menu in country districts.

The main course takes some time to prepare, but the Greeks do not object to this as they adore their food. Eating is not merely for sustenance. One of its essential functions is to offer the opportunity for talking; this is quite simply the Greek national pastime.

Aperitifs and starters

Firstly, as an aperitif you drink an *ouzo*, an aniseed spirit which is clear when poured but which turns milky when mixed with water. Although it goes down well undiluted, ouzo should be treated with respect. It has a fairly high alcohol content and may have an unexpected effect. However, a small glass is very beneficial and prepares the palate and stomach for the starter. In small tavernas this may only be salad or, more precisely, the basic ingredients of a salad: tomatoes, cucumber, peppers, olives and fetta cheese. This is all cut up rather roughly into chunks, swimming in olive oil and not mixed or tossed. Salt, pepper and yet more oil are to be found on the table. The salad is eaten with thickly sliced bread, and cold water, which is safe to drink everywhere, is provided to quench your thirst. The starter (*mezes*) can develop into a tasty hors d'oeuvre, consisting of a selection of the following: taramosalata, aubergine salad, sardines, black and green olives, scampi, mussels, eggs in mayonnaise, and salami.

Soups

After this you need something soothing in the form of lemon soup (*suppa avgolémeno*), a cream of chicken soup (or a consommé) made with egg yolk, cream and lemon juice; or a bean soup (*fassoláda*) to which are added oil, celeriac and carrots. Various fish soups, which are available in the ports, are like French *bouillabaisse* a main meal in themselves. *Magirítsa* is a soup made from offal.

Entrées

The entrées are mostly of obvious Italian origin.

Maccaronia me saltsa: pasta in a tomato sauce, possibly with minced meat (alla bolognese).

Maccaronia (pastitsio) me kima: pasta with minced meat, tomatoes and onions, topped with cheese or béchamel sauce, then baked.

Maccaronia special: as above but with chopped liver, ham and peas.

Moússaka: a layered pie made with aubergines, minced meat and puff pastry, sprinkled with cheese and covered in a béchamel sauce, and baked.

Keftédes: small balls of minced beef baked in fat.

Gívos: keftédes roasted on skewers.

Suzugákia: minced meat formed into cigar-like shapes, fried in hot oil and served with a spicy sauce made from ouzo, onions, tomatoes and peppers.

Biftékia: hamburger.

Ghiouvalákia: minced meat with rice, cooked in stock and sprinkled with lemon juice.

Souvlákia: kebabs.

Dolmádes: rice and minced meat mixed together and cooked in vine leaves.

Vodino stivádo: goulash with rice and baby onions.

Anticipating their meal at a taverna

Octopus hanging on the line

Meat dishes

Arni souvlákia: The Greek national dish, lamb or mutton, has not changed since the time of Homer. The meat is grilled over an open fire; in the country over a wood fire, which gives the meat a delicious flavour.

Kotópulo: chicken;   *gurunópulo*: sucking pig.

Moschári: veal;   *vodíno*: beef.

Kokorétsi: a mixture of offal grilled slowly on an upright spit (not to everyone's taste).

Kolokíthia gemista: courgettes stuffed with meat and rice and baked in the oven with a lemon sauce.

Fish and seafood

The Aegean is not well stocked with fish. Therefore fish is expensive and only available on the coast, and should be eaten when it is very fresh; then it is delicious.

Barbúnia: red mullet; *sinágridka*: sea bream; *garides*: prawns; *kalamarákia*: squid; *oktápodi*: octopus.

Desserts

The desserts (*gliká*) betray their oriental origin. They are all very sweet but very good.

It must be pointed out that *glikó* is not just a dessert but a ritual form of welcome;

it is offered to the guest with a glass of water, especially in the monasteries, and should not be refused, even if it merely consists of sticky custard.

Báklava: thin pastry filled with sugar, nuts and almonds, and soaked in honey.

Galatópita: a kind of semolina cake filled with custard.

Búgatsa: pastry filled with a mixture of cream, flour and sugar.

Cheese
Local cheeses are made from sheep's and goat's milk and are prepared differently in each region. There is a surprising variety of flavours.

Coffee
The meal finishes with coffee. The increasing number of tourists has led to the visitor's being served with instant coffee even when it has not been ordered. To avoid this ask for Greek (Turkish) coffee, *elleniko*. This is prepared individually and boiled with sugar. *Skétos* is without sugar, *métrios* medium sweet, *glikó* sweet.

Drinks
Good beer is available throughout Greece. The better tavernas and all restaurants have a number of good to excellent white, rosé and red wines. Wine from the barrel is only rarely obtainable, but it is well worth asking· for. The traditional drink is *retsina*, the resinated local wine which is by far the cheapest. It owes its existence to practical necessity: the ancient Greeks had neither bottles nor barrels, so they carried the wine in goatskin containers or large clay vessels which were painted with resin from the Aleppo pine to strengthen them. At the same time the resin prevented fermentation which could otherwise easily take place in such unsterilised containers, and this helped to preserve the wine. The practical need for this no longer exists, but the Greeks have become accustomed to the taste.

Meatballs with egg and lemon sauce
(Youvarlákia me saltsa avgolémeno)

For 5 people: 1 lb minced veal, ½ cup white wine, ½ cup water, 1 egg, 1 cup breadcrumbs, 1 teasp. salt, pepper, 3 cups veal stock, chopped parsley.

Mix together all the ingredients except the stock and the parsley. Bring the stock to the boil. Form the mixture into small balls and put into the stock. Simmer gently for 10 minutes. Remove from the stock and keep warm on a plate. Strain the stock and reserve for the sauce.

Sauce: 2 dessertsp. flour, 2 dessertsp. melted butter, 2 eggs, lemon juice. Mix the flour with the melted butter. Add the stock and cook until the sauce thickens. Beat the 2 egg yolks with 4 dessertsp. of lemon juice; add this to the hot sauce, beating it well. Simmer for 2 minutes over a low heat, stirring all the time.

Pour the sauce over the meatballs and garnish with parsley.

Greek dancers in the Delphina Taverna

Tourism

Since the end of the Second World War tourism has developed dramatically. About one million tourists (10% of the total number going to Greece) visit Rhodes annually. In 1989 there were 40,000 hotel beds of every category available. With the exception of the two Alpine hotels on Profitis Ilias, which are only open in summer, all hotels are situated in the capital, on the west coast (as far as Trianda and Kremasti), and on the east coast (Kalithea and Faliraki). There are also two hotels on the bay 3.5 km from Lindos. Other accommodation is available in small pensions and private rooms.

The hotels in the town have the advantage of good transport facilities; on the other hand they have the disadvantage of being noisy. This is due partly to traffic and partly to the music from the tavernas or in the hotels themselves.

Tourism on Kos has developed more recently and the island has only about one third as many visitors as Rhodes. Kos is not only smaller but quieter; nevertheless it offers all the facilities that visitors expect.

Dodecanese fisherman

Hints for your holiday

There is one word in Greek which means both stranger and guest: *xenos*. A stranger is a guest and is treated as one — if he behaves accordingly, that is, like a guest. If he offends against the customs of the country, on the other hand, then he provokes *xenophobia*, dislike of foreigners. In general the Greeks are extraordinarily friendly towards strangers or guests. So it goes without saying: be friendly too!

In recent years Greek tourism has developed very quickly, in some places too quickly. A result of this is that there are not enough staff in some hotels, especially in those of a lower category. It is no use complaining. You are on holiday and have plenty of time. The Mediterranean way of life is different from ours. In the event of a serious complaint you can, of course, contact the hotel reception or tour company, but you can take it for granted that goodwill is always intended.

Certain taboos should be observed: nude sunbathing is forbidden throughout Greece and can lead to heavy fines. Topless sunbathing is usually quietly tolerated on the beaches of Rhodes and Kos. Do not walk around the streets dressed in swimwear. Possession of and dealing in drugs carry severe penalties. Antique objects can only be exported with special permission, even if they have been legally acquired. When visiting churches and monasteries dress decently and behave respectfully. It is best to avoid discussions about Greek politics. Should you wish to photograph Greeks ask them first — they seldom object. Be careful about drinking and remember that Greeks are insulted by the sight of somebody who is very drunk. In common with other Mediterranean races the Greeks themselves only drink at mealtimes, and then only modestly. But all this is obvious. The stranger is not the master but the guest, even when he is paying. The Greeks like the friendly guest — and you will not find it difficult to like the Greeks. They make it easy for the *xenos*, the stranger, the guest.

Mandraki Harbour, Rhodes

Where to go and what to see

The Island of Rhodes

Each year about a million tourists visit Rhodes, simply because Rhodes is a marvellous place. Lamartine wrote: 'Nowhere in the world have I seen a more beautiful sky or more fertile land,' and the books written in praise of Rhodes would almost fill a library.

Rhodes does not have the harsh, rather austere beauty of the Cyclades. The island is an orchard, an oasis, a paradise. It is brilliant like its oranges, fresh like its lemons, blossoming like the hibiscus bushes and the bougainvillaea which cascades over the walls, and scented with thyme, myrtle, coriander and a thousand other aromatic herbs. Sandy beaches invite you to swim; rocky bays tempt you to dive; in the valley of Petaloudes clouds of butterflies dance.

The only bare spot is the *Atavyros*, the 1200-m-high summit of the island; the *Profitis Ilias*, 400 m lower, is thickly forested. The two mountain hotels are called *Elafos* (stag) and *Elafina* (hind), for deer have been indigenous on Rhodes since antiquity. They were brought over from Asia Minor to control the snakes which, according to another story, gave the island its name (the Phoenician word 'rod' means snake). They freed Rhodes of the plague of snakes and became its emblem. This is why a stag and a hind guard the entrance to the harbour.

The reafforestation begun under Italian administration (1912–1944) has shown astonishing results. Vast areas of Rhodes and Kos are wooded again today — quite a rarity in the Aegean. You can witness breathtaking sunsets, and, if you get up early enough, sunrises as well, and you can take part in delightful folk festivals.

No other island in the Aegean can be reached as easily as Rhodes, and on no other can you stay so comfortably. It has accommodation of every type to meet every requirement and to suit all pockets. In the hotels the food is international; in the tavernas it is Greek, Turkish, Oriental and Italian.

Since time immemorial the hospitality of Rhodes has been a byword. Zeus, the father of the gods, saw to that, and today the Greeks still receive visitors in the same way. If you stop in front of a house on Rhodes or admire a garden, it is not unusual to be invited in. Do not hesitate to accept; the invitation is meant to be taken seriously. Even if you cannot communicate, a smile is international. You will probably be offered sweetmeats or coffee, and the lady of the house may present you with a hibiscus flower when you leave. The thing to say is *'efkharistó'* (thank you), a word which is known to Christians through the celebration of the Eucharist, the meal of thanksgiving.

Festivals and Events
On Rhodes

If you are spending more than a week on Rhodes, do not forget to visit one of the Greek folk festivals which take place at various locations on the feast days of local saints. The festivities generally begin on the eve of the feast day itself.

March/April: Easter is the principal festival. Even today Lent is still strictly observed, the fasting becoming more stringent as Easter approaches. In contrast the Easter feasting seems all the more lavish. Processions take place on Good Friday and Easter Saturday; on Easter Sunday midnight mass is held in front of the church. Not until the Easter message has been given in the church are the candles lit from the priest's Easter candle, and the light is passed on from person to person. Easter heralds the start of the new ecclesiastical year and is celebrated with fireworks and fire crackers. In the Orthodox Church the date of Easter is still calculated according to the Julian calendar and so does not always coincide with the date of our Easter.

April 23rd:	*St George* (Kritinia).
May 1st:	*May Day*; the young men make garlands and hang them on their sweethearts' doors. The garlands usually remain in place until July 24th, sometimes even longer.
June 24th:	*St John the Baptist*; celebrated everywhere with bonfires.
June 29th:	*St Peter and St Paul* (Lindos).
July 17th:	*St Mary* (Paradissi).
July 20th:	*Prophet Elias* (Mount Elias — Profitis Ilias).
July 30th:	In honour of *St Saul* (who does not exist in the official Church calendar) a big celebration is held at Soroni. Saul is said to have been a companion of St Paul and to have performed miracles.
August 6th:	*Ascension of Christ* (Maritsa).
August 15th:	*The Virgin Mary* (Kremasti; Embona).
August 23rd:	*The Virgin Mary* (Kremasti; Trianda).
September 8th:	*The Virgin Mary* (Zambiko Monastery).
September 14th:	*The Holy Cross* (Kalithies; Malona).
October 18th:	*St Luke* (Afandou).
October 26th:	*St Demetrios*; also the day on which the new wine is sampled.

In Rhodes town

Son et Lumière, an audio-visual interpretation of the rise and fall (through the siege of 1522) of the Crusaders' town. The changing illumination of the *Grand Master's Palace* is impressive. Performances are given in a number of languages (a different language each evening). Entrance opposite the new market. Performances of traditional folk dancing and singing are presented by the Dimolou group in the Old Town.

The National Theatre, at Mandraki Harbour, hosts plays and ballets which are based on folk customs; for example 'The Rhodian Wedding', 'The Departure of the Sponge Fishermen', etc. Visiting companies from the National Theatre in Athens and the Athenian Festival give performances during the season.

Shopping

In order to help their economic recovery after the destruction caused by the war, the Dodecanese islands were granted a series of tax concessions after liberation. For example, imported foreign spirits are quite cheap. Foreign (especially British) textiles are also relatively inexpensive. Suits and coats are made up surprisingly quickly, but the quality of the finish and workmanship does not always match that of the cloth.

If it is first-class quality and workmanship you are looking for in such items, then perhaps you should think twice before shopping on Rhodes, despite the often tempting prices. Everyday articles, on the other hand, are quite good value.

Jewellery. There is a long tradition of handmade jewellery on Rhodes. Good pieces, copied from traditional designs, are still produced today.

Souvenirs of every description can be bought in Rhodes town, at the harbour, in the Old City, and in Lindos.

Sponges are offered for sale at the harbour and on the island of Symi.

Records of Greek folk music can be found in Socrates Street, in the New Market Hall at Mandraki Harbour and in the New Town.

Carpets and woven goods in traditional patterns are still handmade on Rhodes, especially in the area around Afandou and Archangelos on the east coast.

Handwoven textiles made of wool and silk or of pure silk, woven according to ancient Greek patterns, and decorated with hand-embroidered gold borders based on ancient Byzantine patterns, are available in various shops in the Old Town of Rhodes, particularly in Socrates Street and Museum Square.

Hand-embroidered blouses and *batik work* in traditional styles can be found in Socrates Street in Rhodes Old Town, and in the New Town.

Icons, manufactured using traditional techniques and with ancient motifs, are to be found in the Old Town as well as in many other resorts on the island.

Copperwork and *olivewood carvings* can be found in Rhodes Old Town, especially in Socrates Street.

Ceramics have a long tradition on Rhodes. In Lindos especially, it used to be the custom for every returning sailor to bring his bride or family decorated plates from all over the world. In the shipowners' houses on Lindos you can still see entire walls decorated with plates. They are not for sale, of course, although they have influenced the local pottery, which has adopted many foreign motifs. 'Rhodian plates' are therefore a charming combination of ancient and foreign, especially oriental, styles.

Decorating pottery near Lindos

A Lindos street

On the road to Lindos and in the town itself there are many interesting potteries. The 'Nassos' pottery, situated on the west coast in Paradissi on the Kamiros road, is worth a visit. Here you can watch the women potters at work.

Sports and Games

Watersports take pride of place on Rhodes. Although sharks have not been sighted off the island within living memory, their existence cannot be entirely ruled out, and swimmers are advised to swim parallel to the coast and not venture too far out to sea.

 All the beaches on the north-west and west sides of the island (towards Miramare-Trianda) are free, and most consist of sand and pebbles. The almost constant *meltemi* (north-west wind) means that here you can enjoy swimming among waves (sometimes quite high ones) — a rare pleasure in the Aegean.

The bathing beaches along the east coast all have attractive settings:

Kalithea, 10 km south of Rhodes, is a very romantic sandy bay surrounded by rocks. There is a regular bus service from the town.

Faliraki, 18 km south of the town, has a marvellous sandy beach which slopes gently and is very suitable for non-swimmers and children. There are tavernas, changing cabins, parasols, sun loungers and facilities for sports. You can easily spend the whole day here. There is a regular bus service from Rhodes.

The sandy beaches of *Ladiko, Afandou, Kolimbia, Tsambika Beach* and *Haraki* (all to the east of the Lindos road) are still unspoilt and attractive. Unfortunately most can only be reached by private transport or motorboat. There is a regular bus service between Archangelos, Afandou and Lindos.

It must be emphasised that the sun on Rhodes can be extremely dangerous. To avoid getting sunburnt, return to the shade of a parasol as soon as possible after swimming. The indirect rays reflected from water and sand will brown you more slowly, but the tan will last longer.

Nude bathing is officially prohibited throughout Greece.

Sub-aqua diving is not allowed off the beaches in Rhodes. The Greek authorities want to protect the antique treasures still lying on the seabed.

 Pedalos can be hired on most beaches.

 Almost all beach hotels of category A and luxury class have tennis courts. Enquire at hotel reception. The *Tennis Club of Rhodes* has courts for hire to non-members. Enquire at the club.

 The *Afandou Golf Club*, about 20 km from Rhodes, has an 18-hole course of 6135 m for men and 5540 m for women. There is a clubhouse with showers.

 By donkey to the Acropolis at Lindos.

 Seawater *swimming pools* are to be found at most of the large hotels.

Waterskiing

 Many hotels on the east and west coasts have a minigolf course. There are also minigolf courses in Rhodes Town (near the Palm Hotel), and on the west coast (near the Metropolitan Capsis Hotel), where visitors not staying in hotels can play.

 At all main beaches.

 Windsurfing schools on the west coast, at Faliraki Beach and near the Lindos Bay Hotel.

S Yachts (motorised) can be hired but only with a crew, owing to the dangerous seas. Information from the sailing club at Mandraki Harbour.

The Town of Rhodes

Rhodes town (pop. 42,000 approx.) lies on the north-eastern tip of the island. It consists of two quite distinct areas: the Old Town, surrounded by mighty walls and containing the Knights' and Turkish quarters, and the New Town, built during the Italian administration.

Although the magnificently restored Knights' quarter is the real attraction of the town, on entering the so-called Turkish quarter, where hardly any Turks live today, you find a quiet world of sleepy backstreets with Byzantine churches and Turkish mosques.

In sharp contrast is the bustling, noisy New Town, where many of the hotels are situated.

(The letters in brackets refer to the town map of Rhodes on page 48.)

A tour of the town

The Knights' quarter

If you enter through the *Eleftherias Gate* (Gate of Liberty) (**a**), near Mandraki Harbour, opposite the New Market, you first arrive at the remains of a *Temple of Aphrodite* (**b**), dating from the 3rd c. B.C. Opposite is the *Municipal Gallery*, housing works by modern Greek artists. In the picturesque Symi Square stand the *Old Hospital* (**c**), the *Museum of Folk Art* and the *Inn of the Knights of Auvergne* (**d**). The street then leads to *Museum Square*, from which the Street of the Knights (Greek: *Ippoton*) leads off. In Museum Square stand the *New Hospital of the Knights* (**e**), which nowadays houses the *Archaeological Museum* (see page 51), the reconstructed *House of the English Knights* (**f**), and — opposite the Street of the Knights — the Byzantine *Church of the Madonna (Enderum Mosque)* (**g**).

Italian archaeologists removed all the Turkish additions from the *Street of the Knights* and restored it splendidly, with the result that today it presents what must be unique in Europe, a complete residential street in late Gothic style. The Inns were built about 1500. On the right side of the street (in the direction of the Grand Master's Palace) are the Inns of Italy (**h**), France (**i**) and Provence (**k**); the left side consists chiefly of the Hospital of the Knights and its garden; near the chapter building which spans the street is the large Inn of Spain (**l**). The national groups gathered to consult in the chapter house. The Inn of Germany has not been identified.

The Street of the Knights ends at the *Grand Master's Palace* (**m**) which was constructed in the middle of the 14th c. It was blown up by a gunpowder explosion in 1856 (lightning hit a previously undiscovered gunpowder store dating from the time of the Crusades), and it was rebuilt as a governor's palace during the 1930s by the Italians. As the old palace had been almost completely destroyed, they had to follow old drawings, so it is not an exact replica but rather as close a copy as possible. The palace ruins, together with the ruins of other castles of the Knights of St John on Rhodes and other islands (especially Kos), were used for building material. Whereas the exterior still conveys an impression of the original palace, the interior has been designed throughout in the pompous style of Italian fascism. The Hellenistic mosaics brought here from Kos are well worth seeing.

The whole complex of the Grand Master's Palace is a fortress in itself within the mighty walls of Rhodes. At certain times it is possible to walk along the walls (highly recommended). The palace is most impressive when seen from the *Gate of Amboise* in the west. The gate is named after the French Grand Master d'Amboise (1505–1512). The *Church of St John*, which used to stand opposite the Grand Master's

The Street of the Knights

Palace, and was converted into a mosque by the Turks, was blown up in the same explosion as the palace. It was rebuilt as the Church of the Evangelist at Mandraki Harbour under the Italian administration.

The Turkish quarter

A few steps south of the Grand Master's Palace you are in a completely different world — in the Turkish quarter, which until 1523 was known as the traders' quarter or Greek quarter, and which is once again inhabited by Greeks.

Sultan Suleiman Mosque (**n**) was originally built in 1523 by Sultan Suleiman to show his gratitude for the conquest of Rhodes. Its present-day appearance dates from 1808. The mosque, which is the largest in Rhodes and the only one still used for worship,

does not compare with the Suleiman mosque in Istanbul, the most magnificent mosque in that city. However, if you have not seen a mosque before then the one in Rhodes is well worth a visit.

A short distance in a westerly direction is the *Turkish Library* (**o**) containing valuable Turkish and Arab manuscripts. It is housed in the rooms of the *Medresse Mosque* which used to be a Greek church (St George's) and it has an unusual clover-leaf plan. The pleasant courtyard of the library is decorated with pretty pebble mosaics.

If it is your first visit to this quarter, then return to the harbour via *Socrates Street*, which runs parallel to the Street of the Knights. It is a charming thoroughfare, with many bazaars

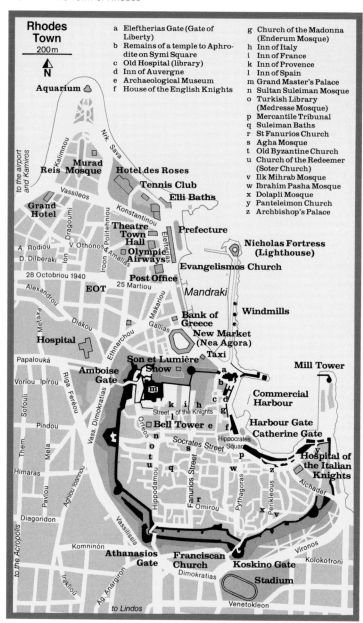

Rhodes Town

200m

N

a Eleftherias Gate (Gate of Liberty)
b Remains of a temple to Aphrodite on Symi Square
c Old Hospital (library)
d Inn of Auvergne
e Archaeological Museum
f House of the English Knights
g Church of the Madonna (Enderum Mosque)
h Inn of Italy
i Inn of France
k Inn of Provence
l Inn of Spain
m Grand Master's Palace
n Sultan Suleiman Mosque
o Turkish Library (Medresse Mosque)
p Mercantile Tribunal
q Suleiman Baths
r St Fanurios Church
s Agha Mosque
t Old Byzantine Church
u Church of the Redeemer (Soter Church)
v Ilk Mihrab Mosque
w Ibrahim Pasha Mosque
x Dolapli Mosque
y Panteleimon Church
z Archbishop's Palace

Aquarium

to the airport and Kamiros

Murad Reis Mosque

Hotel des Roses

Tennis Club

Elli Baths

Grand Hotel

Theatre
Town Hall

Prefecture

Olympic Airways

Post Office

Nicholas Fortress (Lighthouse)

Evangelismos Church

A. Rodiou
D. Dilberaki

28 Octobriou 1940

25 Martiou

EOT

Mandraki

Windmills

Bank of Greece

New Market (Nea Agora)

Hospital

Mill Tower

Taxi

Son et Lumière Show

Amboise Gate

Commercial Harbour

Street of the Knights

Bell Tower

Harbour Gate
Catherine Gate

Socrates Street

Hippocrates Square

Hospital of the Italian Knights

Franciscan Church

Athanasios Gate

Koskino Gate

Stadium

to Lindos

to the Acropolis

Kalimmou
Vassileos
Konstantinou
Vassileos
Dragoumi
Politehniou
Iroon Politehniou
Amalias
Eleftheias
Makariou
Gallias
Ethnarchou
Nik. Sava
V. Othonos
Ion
Alexandrou
Metaxa
Diákou
Papalouká
Riga Feréou
Voriou Ipírou
Sofouli
Pindou
Them.
Mela
Pavlou
Himaras
Diagoridon
Aghiou Ioannou
Orfeos
Hippodamou
Vass. Dimokratias
Vassilissis
Fanurios Street
Omirou
Komninón
Ag. Anargiron
Traklioú
Dimokratias
Venetokleon
Pythagoras
Perikleous
Alchader
Vironos
Kolokotroni

selling a vast array of art and junk. It leads to the *fishmarket* and to the fine building of the former *Mercantile Tribunal* (Castellania 1507) (**p**). You then pass through Ermou Street to the impressive *Harbour Gate* which dominates the *Knights' Harbour*, where cargo boats and pleasure cruisers now berth.

Around the Old Town

If you have both the time and the inclination, then you should not be satisfied with this one tour, but set aside a few hours to return to the Old Town south of Socrates Street. Time seems to have stood absolutely still here. Unfortunately the Old Town was quite badly damaged by bombing in the Second World War, so that some parts are almost devastated. Parts of the ancient town were exposed by the bombs, so the archaeologists halted reconstruction until all the results of the excavations had been assessed.

In the Turkish quarter are the magnificent *Turkish Baths* (Suleiman Baths) (**q**) which were similarly destroyed but have been rebuilt and are again in use. They can be reached from the Suleiman Mosque via Hippodamou Street and Archelaos Street. Next to the Turkish Baths is the *Mustafa Mosque* of 1765. The majority of mosques are adapted Byzantine churches dating from the time of the Crusades. Unfortunately they are without exception in a poor state of repair; even the partly exposed frescos are scarcely recognisable. Most churches and mosques are closed but a walk through the maze of streets in the Old Town is well worth while, especially for photographers. You may take a wrong turning, but it does not

The sea-horse fountain

matter as you will always come up against the town walls which surround the Turkish quarter, or find yourself in Socrates Street again, so it is impossible to get lost.

Important churches and mosques: *St Fanurios Church (Pial-ed-Tin Mosque)* (**r**) in Fanurios Street, which crosses Socrates Street, was built in 1335 and has some partially preserved frescos; services are held every Sunday, and August 27th is the feast of St Fanurios. The *Agha Mosque* (**s**) was badly damaged during the war but has been rebuilt. West of Hippodamou Street are the *Old Byzantine Church* (**t**) and the *Church of the Redeemer* (Soter Church) (**u**). On Pericles Street below the walls is the *Ilk Mihrab Mosque* (**v**), a Byzantine church with frescos dating

from the 14th c., and near St Fanurios Church in a large square stands the *Rejeb Mosque* (1588) which is in very bad condition. North-east of the Rejeb Mosque in Pythagoras Street you will find the *Ibrahim Pasha Mosque* (**w**), built in 1531. Demosthenes Street brings us to the *Dolapli Mosque* (**x**), formerly the principal church, and one of the oldest Byzantine churches on Rhodes. It was destroyed in 1943, rebuilt after the war, and now once again serves the Christian community. On the eastern edge of the Knights' Harbour, where land- and sea-walls meet, stands the *Panteleimon Church* (**y**), and a short way to the west on Pindar Street are the *Hospital of the Italian Knights* (1516), the Gothic *Church of St Mary* and, opposite

Entrance to the Hospital of the Knights

Pericles Street, the *Archbishop's Palace* (**z**) with the much photographed sea-horse fountain in front of it. From here head back to Mandraki Harbour, along either the inside or the outside of the harbour walls. The only mosque not in the Old Town is the *Murad Reis Mosque,* dating from 1523, with a picturesque Turkish cemetery. This is situated on the northern tip of Rhodes, near the Hotel des Roses.

If you start at the *Amboise Gate* and head south, you will come to the following *bastions* which were each allocated to a national group for defence: Germany — *St George's Tower;* Auvergne — the *Spanish Tower;* Spain — *Mary's Tower* (through which the Turks entered and which they walled up in 1531 so that the same fate did not befall them); England — between the *Athanasios Gate* and *Koskino Gate;* Provence — *Caretto Bastion;* Italy — the remaining section to the top of the harbour; Castile — the harbour; France — the section north of the Amboise Gate.

The Acropolis of Rhodes
(Monte Smith)

The ancient town was about four to five times the size of that of the present day and spread like an amphitheatre up towards Monte Smith, formerly called Monte San Stefano and renamed after a British General.

The Acropolis can be reached by bus, or in about half an hour on foot from the Athanasios Gate via Komninon Street, or from the Amboise Gate along Vass. Dimokratias and Aghiou Ioannou Streets to Diagoridon Street.

Italian architects identified the remains of a temple of Zeus Polieus and Athena (Polias) on the acropolis and partially rebuilt a *Temple of Apollo Pythios* (Doric; 3rd c. B.C.). Below the Temple of Apollo is the heavily restored 2nd c. *Odeion,* an open-air auditorium for teachers of rhetoric; next to it is the

Marble Stadium also restored by the Italians.

Monte Smith offers an excellent view over the whole north-west coast. It is best to visit it in the evening when you can enjoy breathtaking sunsets which are exceptionally fine on Rhodes.

The New Town

All the important buildings in the New Town, which was built by the Italians (chiefly by the architect del Fausto), are located at Mandraki Harbour, the biggest of Rhodes' three harbours: the *New Market* (Nea Agora) with its many shops; the *Bank of Greece;* the *Post Office;* the *Prefecture* (formerly the Italian governor's palace); the *Town Hall;* the *National Theatre* and the *Evangelismos Church* (Church of the Annunciation) with new wall paintings in traditional Byzantine style.

On the northern tip of the island is the pretty *Aquarium,* built of shell limestone, which provides a good general survey of the wildlife of the Aegean.

The offices of shipping companies and travel agencies are to be found in the New Town. The information office of the Greek Tourist Organisation (EOT) is situated at the end of Amerikis Street.

  For art-lovers

A visit to the *Archaeological Museum* in the New Knights' Hospital (Museum Square behind the Street of the Knights) is strongly recommended. The building was begun in 1440 when the old hospital (now a library, in Symi Square) became too small, and it was completed in 1489. It is a pure example of late Gothic architecture. First you enter the courtyard, almost 1000 sq. m in size, and enclosed on all sides by arcades. Large amphoras and a splendid lion (1st c. B.C.) are displayed there, and pyramids of stone and iron cannonballs are relics of the many

Amphitheatre at the Acropolis of Rhodes

The Archaeological Museum

sieges suffered by the city of Rhodes. Some of the stone balls are said to originate from the siege by Demetrios Poliorketes (305–304 B.C.; see page 17). In the courtyard a broad flight of steps leads to the first floor where the actual museum rooms are situated.

The main hall served as an infirmary ward; the carers slept in the small adjoining chambers which are now closed. The alcove was used as a chapel where mass was said every day. The beamed ceiling is made of dark cypress wood. This exceptionally nobly proportioned room still houses only tombstones of the knights 'fallen for the honour of the Lord'.

The statues are exhibited in the rooms to the south of the infirmary ward and in the garden courtyard, while the north rooms house one of the biggest collections of vases in Greece. It may not match the one in the National Museum in Athens but it contains good examples from all the important epochs. As the rooms are quite small you are never overwhelmed but can concentrate quietly on one style at a time.

The most significant pieces in the sculpture collection are: two Archaic *kouroi* (adolescents) from the 6th c. B.C.; the *grave stele of Tamarista* (about 400 B.C.), a work of classical beauty, in which all the pain of the final parting is expressed with restrained sorrow; the *Marine Venus* (4th c.) to which Lawrence Durrell devoted so many inspired pages; the delightful little *Aphrodite of Rhodes*, who is holding her hair out to dry it, as if she has just stepped out of the bath (about 100 B.C., a marble copy of a late Classical original in bronze); and the head of *Helios* (2nd c. B.C.), which possibly gives an idea of what the head of the gigantic Helios statue (Colossus of Rhodes) looked like.

For archaeological sites and churches see Excursions (page 54).

Lion statue in the museum courtyard

Grave stele of Tamarista in the museum

▶◀ Evenings out

In Rhodes you can spend your evenings in many ways. You can sample Greek specialities in a taverna or try the delicacies of other specialist restaurants; you can dance until early morning in discothèques or visit folk festivals. Everywhere there are pleasant places where you can sit and have a glass of wine and a chat.

🍴 *Kontiki*, the floating restaurant by the harbour jetty. *Vlachos*, Monte Smith, Greek cuisine. *Dania*, near the TUI office, cold Danish buffet every Sunday evening. *Maison Fleurie*, in the New Town on the Lindos road, French cuisine. *Captain's House*, near the Blue Sky Hotel, international and Greek cuisine. *Sierra del Paella*, near the aquarium, fish restaurant. *Mandy's*, near the Hotel Ibiscus/Mediterranean, Chinese cuisine.

Tavernas in the Old Town

Casa Castellana, steak house. *Plaka*, on Hippocrates Square, good fish cuisine. *Tsambiko*, in the market hall, Greek and international cuisine. *Alexis*, Socrates Street, fish specialities. *Argo*, fish restaurant. *Fotis*. *Pythagoras*, Pythagoras Street. *Melas*, near the Grand Master's Palace, very good Greek cuisine.

Greek tavernas out of town

Vrachos, *Trata* and *Kaliva*, all near the Hotel Golden Beach, fresh fish specialities. *Ta Kupia*, Konaki in the village of Tris. *Gefyra*, in Pastida. *Lihoudies* (Cypriot), towards Faliraki. *Konfas*, opposite the airport.

🍷 *Izabella*, in the Grand Hotel Astir Palace. *Tropican*, in the Hotel Rhodos Palace. *Rhodian Cellar*, in the Park Hotel. *Spilia*, Hotel Rhodos Bay. *Hotel Golden Beach*. *Number One*, Hotel Metropolitan Capsis. *CBS (Come Back Soon)*, Hotel Faliraki Beach.

Safari Club, Hotel Paradise, Kalithea.
Bouzouki Cafés (10 p.m.–2 a.m.), expensive and noisy: *Minuit*, at the Palm Hotel. *Copacabana*, at Acandia harbour, an international programme and bouzouki music after midnight. *Rhodos by night*, *Iphigenia*, near the Hotel Miramare.

Greek Music

Amoni, in the Hotel El Greco, well known Rhodian singers. *Zorbas*, near TUI office (Iroon Politechniou Street), Greek music. *Blue Bird* and *Blue Note* in Alexandrou Diakou Street.

Casino

In the Grand Hotel Astir Palace, Roulette, Baccara and Black Jack (17+4).

🎵 Mainly for young people

Aquarius, at Monte Smith, 9 p.m.– 2 a.m. *Mike's Pub*, in an old villa. *Babylon*, also at Monte Smith. *Tongo*, near TUI office, Othonos Amalias Street (no dancing). *High Way Disco*, near the Hotel Rhodos Palace. *La Scala Disco*, near the Hotel Dionysos. *Barbarossa*, Old Town. *Sticky Finger* in the New Town, live music. *Christos Garden*, Griva Street. *Memories*, Dragonmi Street. *Pink Panther*, on the west coast.

Excursions on Rhodes
Rodini

South of Rhodes town, in the direction of Lindos (10 minutes by bus), lies Rodini, a little village with a park, a valley and cemeteries. In this well watered area the Italians laid out a beautiful shady park with unusual plants, streams and pretty paths. There is a garden restaurant with a nightclub. A path leads to the left past two stone lions into the romantic Rodini valley with old and young cypresses, oleander bushes and agaves. It takes 10 minutes to reach the spring at the end of the

The beach at Rhodes

little valley. Go up towards the left on to a plateau where there is a small road with several grottos. Continue to the right along the cypress-lined track and you will come to a cavern with ancient niches hollowed out for tombs. Beyond the cavern you cross some charming countryside and arrive at the *Tomb of the Ptolemies*. There are, however, no Ptolemies buried here; it is a Hellenistic tomb in a chamber in the rock, with twenty-one Doric half-columns. If you have the time and stout footwear you can walk for several hours along the Rodini valley and will meet very few other people. You can return by bus from Rodini park to the town.

Excursions by bus

Buses for the following places leave from the New Market Hall.

Kalithea

Kalithea lies 10 km south of Rhodes town on the Lindos road. It is a picturesquely situated resort, with a thermal bath established under the Italian administration. The water is drunk to treat gout, kidney and liver disease, and digestive complaints. Hippocrates is supposed to have praised its effectiveness. Destroyed during the Second World War, it was rebuilt but is at present not in use.

Faliraki

Faliraki, 18 km south of Rhodes town and east of the Lindos road, has a wide, flat, sandy beach, with tavernas and changing facilities (see Sports and Games, page 44). During the season there is a regular bus service to Rhodes town, Archangelos, Afandou and Lindos. There is a lot of activity on the beach and good sports facilities

(windsurfing, waterskiing, pedalos etc.). Large hotels and a number of small pensions make Faliraki a good holiday centre.

Lindos Pop. 1500

The most important excursion on the east coast is to Lindos, 56 km south-east of Rhodes town and one of the most beautiful places in the Aegean.

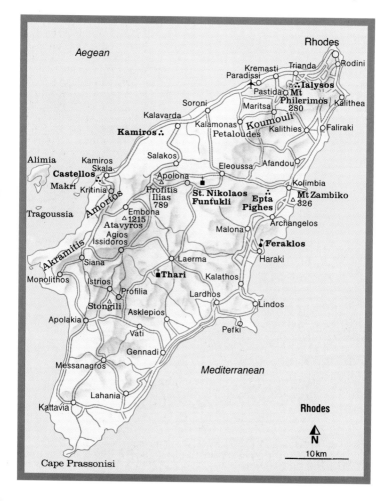

The journey takes about one hour and the route runs parallel to the coast through the picturesque villages of *Afandou*, *Archangelos* and *Malona*. The Acropolis of Lindos can be seen from afar, towering high above the sea on a steep cliff. Lindos was the most important of the three Doric towns on Rhodes and had its heyday under Kleoboulos in the 6th c. B.C. (see page 14). After the founding of the joint capital Rhodos in 408 B.C. Lindos declined in importance, but in the Hellenistic period in the 3rd c. B.C. it acquired the buildings which are so much admired today. Lindos has remained continuously inhabited, unlike the other two towns of Ialysos and Kamiros, and has thus become a living museum. You can ride up to the Acropolis on a donkey (drivers can be found waiting with their animals at the bus station), but you should walk down and explore the attractive little town. The ancient site of the *Acropolis* is enclosed by a formidable castle of the Knights of St John dating from the time of the Grand Master d'Aubusson (1476–1505).

At the entrance to the medieval citadel (**a**) can be seen a 5-m-high ancient relief of a *trireme* (warship with three banks of oars) (**b**) in good condition; it is a monument to a Rhodian sea victory of about 180 B.C. and probably supported the statue of the victorious admiral Hagesandros.

The steps then lead through the mighty Knights' Castle (**c**)–(**d**) to the *castle church* (**e**) and from there to the *Temple Terrace* (**f**) below. This is dominated by a partly restored colonnaded area 88 m wide (Doric; 2nd c. B.C.) which frames the 21-m-wide flight of steps to the upper terrace (**g**). Crossing the courtyard (**h**) you come to the highest point and the colonnaded hall (**i**), 166 m above sea level (take care: the steep drop is not guarded). Here is the *Temple of Athena Lindia* (**j**) which was built about 330 B.C. and which housed a gold and ivory statue of Athena. An older temple dating from the time of Kleoboulos (6th c. B.C.), which stood on the same spot, was destroyed by fire. It was dedicated to Lindia, the goddess of the town of Lindos; the connection with Athena

Lindos

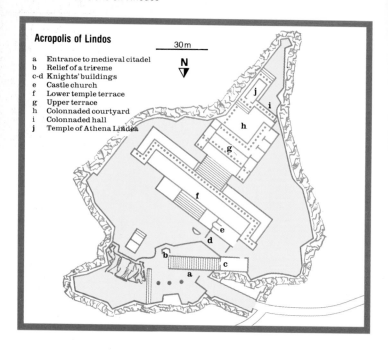

Acropolis of Lindos

30 m

N

a   Entrance to medieval citadel
b   Relief of a trireme
c-d Knights' buildings
e   Castle church
f   Lower temple terrace
g   Upper terrace
h   Colonnaded courtyard
i   Colonnaded hall
j   Temple of Athena Lindea

came about later through Attic influence. The myth concerning the birth of Athena (from the head of Zeus) may have originated in Lindos during the period of Attic rule (5th c.).

A Doric *propylaeon* (doorway) of about 300 B.C., which stood between the colonnaded hall and the temple, no longer exists. In the extreme north of the site is a temple which was built in about A.D. 300 and probably devoted to the cult of emperor-worship.

The apostle Paul is believed to have landed in one of the picturesque rocky coves below the acropolis in A.D. 51. These coves are the only good natural harbours on the island.

On a tour of Lindos you should visit the 15th c. Byzantine *Church of St Mary* with beautiful 18th c. wall paintings, but leave time for a stroll through the picturesque narrow streets with their pebble mosaics. The splendid captains' houses (15th–17th c.) are also worth seeing.

Souvenirs of every kind, especially embroidery, woven articles and ceramics, are on sale; Lindian plates decorated with Greek and Arab motifs are particularly interesting.

Bus excursions on the west coast

On the west coast organised excursions are mainly to Trianda, Petaloudes and Kamiros.

Trianda Pop. 3000

Trianda is situated 15 km south-west of Rhodes. The name comes from *trianda* (thirty) because thirty knights had their summer villas here, although judging by the one which is still standing on the right of the road these were more like castles than country houses. In the

Valley of Butterflies . . .   *. . . and the butterflies*

church of Trianda is a noteworthy iconostasis (screen between nave and altar) carved from olivewood. Also to be seen are some beautiful icons.

Petaloudes

The 'Valley of Butterflies', Petaloudes, lies 26 km south-west of Rhodes. The road diverges from the coast at Paradissi and after passing through Kalamonas reaches the wooded ravine which is filled with luxuriant vegetation and is at a height of 480 m.

The butterflies need quiet in the daytime, but in recent years too many noisy tourists have sought out the valley, with the result that the butterflies' strength has been sapped and their numbers have dropped sharply. If you visit Petaloudes be sure to be as quiet as possible.

Kamiros

Kamiros, the ancient Greek *Kameiros*, 36 km south-west of Rhodes, was probably originally a Cretan settlement; the numerous discoveries from the tombs certainly suggest a close link with Minoan Crete. Later it was inhabited by Dorian Greeks, but owing to its unprotected situation by the sea it did not attain anything like the importance of its sister towns of Lindos and Ialysos. After the founding of the joint capital Rhodes in 408 B.C., Kamiros continued to be inhabited until the 4th c. A.D.

The town, which had completely disappeared and was not rediscovered until the end of the 19th c., when it was partially excavated, offers the unusual sight in Greece of an ancient residential town. Most of the houses date from the Hellenistic period (3rd–2nd c. B.C.) and are reminiscent of the contemporary residential sites on the island of Delos. A large proportion of the pieces on display in the Museum of Rhodes are from the tombs of Kamiros. These consist mainly of vases and the grave stele of Krito and Tamarista.

Kamiros is completely isolated by woods — an amphitheatre surrounded by pine-trees. From the 125-m-high hill on which the acropolis stood, a marvellous view over the countryside and sea can be enjoyed. On this highest point was the Temple of Athena of Kamiros, of which only the foundations remain. In front extended a 200-m-long Doric stoa, six columns of which have been rebuilt. Enormous cisterns (6th c. B.C.) which provided the town's water supply can be seen outside the stoa. In the deepest hollow of the amphitheatre lies the market square, and nearby is a sacred area with the ruins of a temple to Apollo (3rd c. B.C.) and several altars. Between these two public areas the residential town climbs up the side of the hill, bisected by a splendid straight main road.

Since we so often see or visualise

magnificent Greek temples and hardly ever see Greek dwelling houses, it is easy to form the impression that the Greeks themselves were almost demi-gods who strolled about their colonnades like marble figures. Kamiros offers an opportunity to correct this view. The whole town is not much wider than the stoa on the acropolis. The Greeks lived in public — their houses were used for little more than sleeping.

Excursions by car

If you want to see more of Rhodes than you can by joining standard excursions, you will need a car for one or two days (for car hire or taxi see page 90). The following places are worth visiting:

Mt Philerimos

Philerimos lies 14 km south-west of Rhodes. The name means 'friend of loneliness', and whoever stands on the 280-m summit soon understands why. But it has not always been so. The Phoenicians first settled on this dominant point on the west coast; centuries later Mycenaean Greeks founded Achaia here, their first town on Rhodes. In the 11th c. the Dorians conquered the town and renamed it Ialysos after the mythical founder, the son of Kerkaphos and grandson of the sun god Helios (see page 11). On the summit stood the acropolis of the town which in its heyday probably extended as far as Trianda; several graves have been found there. The town itself has not so far been excavated. Diagoras, to whom Pindar dedicated his much quoted ode as a prize for his victory in the Olympic Games of 464 B.C., came from Ialysos. On Philerimos the knights waited for reinforcements, as they could not take Rhodes by surprise attack; two hundred years later Sultan Suleiman also made his preparations for attack from here; finally Philerimos was the scene of the worst fighting

between the Germans and Italians in 1943 during the Second World War.

During the Byzantine period a monastery stood here (the mountain probably got its name at that time); the knights converted it into a Catholic church and on their retreat took with them the miraculous icon of the Virgin Mary. In the Turkish period it fell into decay but the Italians rebuilt it as a Catholic monastery, using the old plans. However, it was again destroyed during the fighting in 1943 and was rebuilt after the war by the Greeks.

In front of the 'Knights' church' are the ruins of a *Temple of Athena* (3rd c. B.C.) and an early Christian font. On the left near the entrance to the monastery grounds is a *Chapel of St George* built into the rock; it contains 15th c. frescos.

Kamiros

A Special Tip
A stepped pathway leads down from the car park to the beautiful Doric fountain-house (about 300 B.C.; restored by the Italians). Here terminate two of the thirteen subterranean paths which the Dorians, following the underground water-course, bored through the mountain. Leave the car park and climb to the right opposite the monastery grounds, following the 'Stations of the Cross' path, laid out by the Italians, which leads to a beautiful viewpoint. The kiosk at the car park sells a speciality of Philerimos – the bitters *Sette Erbe* which is distilled from seven herbs.

Kamiros-Skala Pop. 800
Kamiros-Skala is where the deep-sea fishermen land their catches. This little place was once the harbour for the inland town of Kritinia (originally a Cretan settlement, see page 12). From Kamiros-Skala small boats cross daily to the island of Chalki.

Castellos
To the right of the road tower the ruins of Castellos, a castle of the Knights of St John. It is well worth the climb in order to enjoy the extremely fine views in all directions (15 minutes from the road).

Embona Pop. 700
Via Kritinia the road leads to Embona, a picturesque, unspoilt mountain village among olive groves and vineyards. Red

Monolithos

and white Embona wine is produced here. In the *church* of Embona there is a beautifully carved iconostasis made of gold-embossed olivewood. Traditional costume is still worn here and the dancers are considered to be the best on Rhodes.

Embona lies at the foot of *Atavyros* (1251 m) which can be climbed from here. As Atavyros is completely bare and the path has no shade, it is best to spend the night at Embona and set out about two hours before dawn (lightweight climbing boots or thick-soled rubber shoes are recommended). Sunrise on Atavyros is a memorable sight. From Embona the road winds around Atavyros and leads through a varied landscape to the village of Monolithos.

Monolithos

Monolithos has an interesting church, and if you go on a little further towards Frourion you come to the most southerly of the knights' castles.

The castle stands on a 240-m-high rock cone (monolith). The *Panteleimon Chapel* in the castle has interesting frescos. If you are in Monolithos late in the day wait to see the sun go down because here the sunsets are the most spectacular on Rhodes.

Mt Profitis Ilias

Profitis Ilias is the name usually given to the highest summit on any Greek island because the prophet Elias ascended to heaven from a mountain top. Clearly we are dealing with a Christianised version of Helios, the sun god who drove across the heavens in his sun chariot. As the 'h' is not pronounced in modern Greek, and 'e' sounds like 'i', the switch was a simple one. On Rhodes, however, the highest summit, Atavyros, is associated with Zeus and the second highest with the prophet Elias. It is possible to drive nearly to the top of the 789-m-high peak of Profitis Ilias. The reafforestation introduced by the Italians has been very successful here. The mountain is completely wooded and reminiscent of the lower Alps. There are two hotels, Elafos and Elafina ('stag' and 'hind'), built in the style of Alpine chalets (open only during the summer).

St Nikolaos Funtukli

Continuing towards Eleoussa you come to the small Byzantine *Church of St Nikolaos Funtukli*, which stands alone on an enchanting plateau. If you push back the heavy iron bolts on the three doors you will see a series of wall paintings. The church and frescos were endowed in the 14th or 15th c. by an important administrative official whose

St Nikolaos Funtukli

three children had died as a result of plague. The church was therefore dedicated to St Nicholas, the protector of children. Near one of the doors can be seen a fresco of the donor, his wife and his three children.

Epta Pighes

A good road runs from Eleoussa through fertile and well watered countryside to Epta Pighes, the Seven Springs, which is a popular picnic place with the people of Rhodes. From here it is only a few kilometres to *Kolimbia*, one of the prettiest coves on the east coast.

A Special Tip

From the woodland inn at Epta Pighes you can follow the course of the stream for a short way and then walk alongside the water through a tunnel (about 60 m long) which emerges on the other side of the hill in an idyllic pool. It is advisable to take a torch.

Kolimbia

Kolimbia Bay has a magnificent and romantic white sandy beach, framed by gigantic rocks which have broken off from Mt Zambiko. It is ideal for sunbathers, non-swimmers, swimmers, snorkelers and divers. There is a taverna.

Mt Zambiko

While you are at Kolimbia it is worth making the 1-hour climb up the 326-m-high Mt Zambiko which is crowned by a chapel. The ascent begins about one kilometre from the bay. Turn left onto a little mountain path, which is marked with crosses indicating that the chapel at the summit is a pilgrimage church. Women who have been unable to have a child are said to undertake the pilgrimage, spend a night in the church and eat some candlewick. If they subsequently have a child it is baptised Zambiko if it is a boy and Zambika if it is a girl. There are quite a number of Zambikos and Zambikas on Rhodes! There is a wonderful panoramic view from the summit of Mt Zambiko. The path is chiefly through woods but is rather stony, so light climbing boots or thick-soled rubber shoes are recommended.

Archangelos Pop. 3300

About 7 km south of Kolimbia in the orange-growing area lies Archangelos (carpets and woven goods), the largest village on the island. In spite of attracting many tourists it is still relatively unspoilt. Above the village are the scanty remains of a castle of the Knights of St John. The castle of the same order at *Feraklos*, south of Archangelos near the resort of Charaki, is much better preserved. Feraklos was where the knights first landed when they set out to conquer Rhodes. It was here too, in the fortress which they had greatly improved, that they held out for longest against the Turks. There are beautiful coves and beaches between Feraklos and Lindos.

Asklepios Pop. 600

15 km south-west of Lindos, in the woods a little way inland, lies the hamlet of Asklepios with a whitewashed Byzantine *church* which dates from 1060. It is richly decorated with frescos.

Thari

The monastery of Thari, which is very remotely situated, contains some 12th c. frescos, some of which are well preserved. It is reached by turning inland off the main road at Lardhos (12 km west of Lindos) towards Laerma (good sand road). Enquire in Laerma whether the church is open, or if necessary ask the priest to send someone with a key. From there you turn off to the left and then go along a forest road (passable with care) to Thari. It is well worth the journey. According to legend Thari was founded by a Byzantine princess in gratitude for the cure she found in the fresh woodland countryside. Thari lies in a clearing in the woods, near a spring where deer come to drink in the evening.

The broad monastery courtyard and the many cells bear witness to the fact that the monastery was once of great importance; nowadays it stands neglected in the solitude of the forest. The return journey is either along the same route to Laerma or along a good sand road, with lovely views into the interior of the island, to Profilia.

Kattavia

In the extreme south of Rhodes, on a plain enclosed by low hills, lies the village of Kattavia which has not yet

A Greek Orthodox priest

Holiday island — Symi

been 'discovered' by tourists. *St Mary's Church*, dating from the 14th c., contains frescos of the 16th–19th c.; the village priest will usually be pleased to unlock the church on request. A 6-km-long minor road leads from Kattavia to the southern tip of the island. The excellent beach here is called *Prassonisi*.

Excursions by boat and plane

There are no boat trips around the island of Rhodes. There are, however, bathing trips every day along the east coast as far as Lindos. There is a choice between motorised sailing vessels and excursion boats. Depending on the vessel in service several stops are made at various beaches, usually in the bays of Ladiko, Afandou, Zambika, Kolimbia (see page 63) and Kalithea (see page 55). Day excursions by ship or hydrofoil are run to Symi, Kos and Patmos and occasionally to Tilos. Visitors can make their own way by ferry or plane to the islands of Kastellorizo, Chalki, Karpathos, Kassos, Nisyros and Kalymnos (see pages 82–87), but it is usually necessary to spend one or two nights there. At present there are no day excursions by boat to Marmaris in nearby Turkey. Greek shopkeepers are wary of competition from Turkish bazaars. There are no important historic buildings in Marmaris but the bazaar in the Old Town and the late medieval castle are interesting. Most of the inhabitants of this popular resort are descended from Turkish emigrants from Crete.

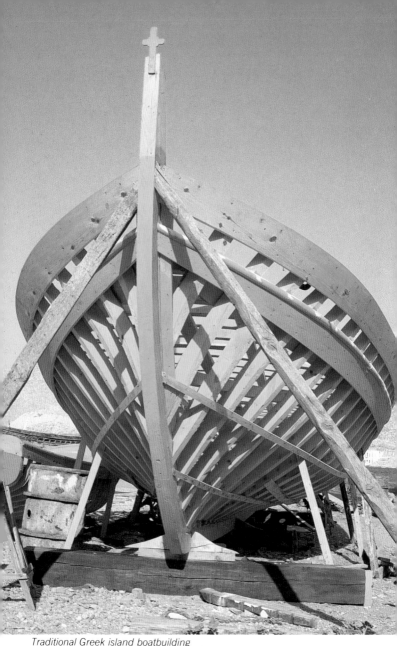

Traditional Greek island boatbuilding

Kos

The Island of Kos

The Ancient Greeks used to say, 'If Kos cannot feed you then neither can Egypt,' to illustrate how fertile the island was. The geographer Strabo, to whom we are indebted for a great deal of important information about Ancient Greece, wrote: 'The town of the Koans is not especially large but it is better to live in than all other towns and it presents a wonderful sight when you sail past.' Diodorus of Sicily added: 'A host of races is gathered within, and magnificent town walls and a notable harbour have been built. So it was that in the course of time the town had considerable public income and private wealth to show, as is the way with cities.'

These quotations all refer to Kos during the Classical and Hellenistic periods. The island's affluence and its inhabitants' feeling of well-being were thus apparent to visitors even in ancient times — and not much has changed up to the present day. This may be the reason why the Koans, in contrast to most of the other island Greeks, preferred to stay at home; many still do. Kos did not take part in the Greek colonisation of the first millennium B.C. In sharp contrast to Rhodes it did not engage in independent politics or bold seafaring. On the contrary the numerous conquests show how desirable the peaceful island always was.

Shopping

Typical products of the island are woven and knitted articles and ceramics. Because of reduced customs duty foreign spirits are relatively cheap.

Ceramic souvenirs

Kos Old Town

Sports and Games

The beaches at Tingaki and Paradise Beach are particularly beautiful but there are also many lovely small beaches elsewhere on the island.

S In the big bathing and sports centre which extends westwards from Kos town to Faros; in Kardamena and in Kefalos Bay.

Throughout the island, particularly on the deserted peninsula south of Kefalos.

Cycling is very popular on Kos as the roads (especially around the town) are quite flat. The Asklepieion, Faros, and the beaches of Tingaki, as well as Cape Psalidi, Cape Fokas and Empros Thermae, are all easily accessible by bicycle.

Climbing is highly recommended on Kos; the climb from Zia to the summit of the 846-m-high Dikeos takes about two hours.

On the hard courts of the hotels.

The Town of Kos

The town of Kos (pop. 12,000 approx.) lies on the northern tip of the island. Its harbour is dominated by the impressive Castle of the Knights of St John. Two extensive burial grounds have been excavated in the centre; these convey an impression of the ancient town.

Kos town has grown rapidly in recent years but it has remained almost a garden town, with its oriental architecture and numerous palms giving it a somewhat African character.

The tourist facilities are situated on the harbour promenade and on the town beach, to the south of the harbour, almost outside the residential area. (The letters in brackets refer to the map of Kos; see page 71.)

 Around the town

Apart from the castle there is considerably more to see of the ancient town than of the medieval one. One reason for this is that the earthquake in 1933 destroyed large parts of the town. Kos was therefore rebuilt, and (as far as the official buildings are concerned) rebuilt in the style preferred by the Italians at that time, which is more evocative of North Africa than of the other Greek islands. However, this allowed the archaeologists the opportunity to make large-scale excavations, which can be seen today.

The centre of the small town is *Eleftherias Square* (Freedom Square) (**a**), which is dominated by the *Defdendar Mosque* (**b**), built in the late 18th c. (closed, shops on the ground floor). Diagonally opposite stands the *Market Hall* (**c**) which is always bustling with activity and where the island's fruits and vegetables are on sale. In contrast the fish market outside the market hall seems rather bare; this is perhaps symptomatic of the now low

Kos

Mosaic in the museum depicting the arrival of Asklepios

Statue of Hippocrates

fish stocks in the Aegean. On the north side of the square is the museum (**d**); between here and the market there is a café which is always crowded and the 'Château' restaurant. Several little streets between the restaurant and the market hall lead into the Old Town, which is in fact not very old, although its crooked narrow streets exude the atmosphere of Greek island architecture. Among the picturesque little houses there are many souvenir shops.

From Eleftherias Square it is only a few steps past the museum to Akti Koundouriotou, the road flanking the whole harbour (which like that in Rhodes is called Mandraki). Many cafés, more international than Greek, stand between the offices of the shipping agencies and a few banks. Here you can sit and chat and watch the activity around the harbour.

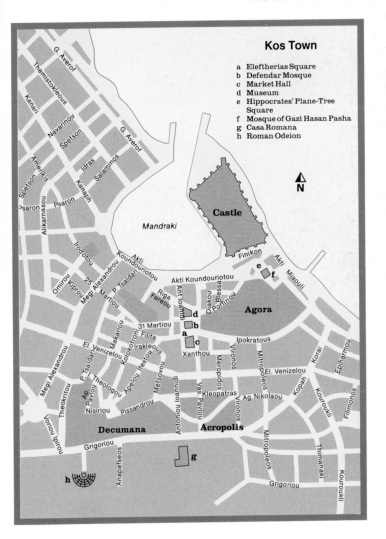

Kos Town

a Eleftherias Square
b Defendar Mosque
c Market Hall
d Museum
e Hippocrates' Plane-Tree Square
f Mosque of Gazi Hasan Pasha
g Casa Romana
h Roman Odeion

The Museum (d)

The museum houses mainly sculptures from Hellenistic and Roman periods. The central hall is shaped like the interior courtyard of a rich Roman villa (see Casa Romana, page 74) and is decorated with a large mosaic in excellent condition which depicts the arrival of Asklepios on the island of Kos (2nd or 3rd c. A.D.). On the right-hand

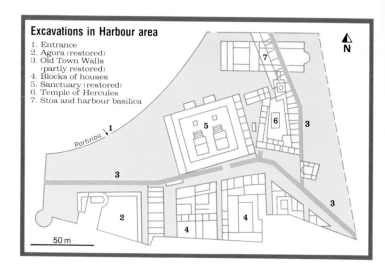

Excavations in Harbour area
1. Entrance
2. Agora (restored)
3. Old Town Walls
   (partly restored)
4. Blocks of houses
5. Sanctuary (restored)
6. Temple of Hercules
7. Stoa and harbour basilica

N

Porfiriou

50 m

side of the picture he is greeted by an islander who is filled with joyful anticipation, as if he already knows what riches Asklepios and his temple are to bring to the island. To the left Hippocrates sits expectantly. Asklepios himself is preparing to cross a narrow gangway to set foot on land. The Italians discovered many excellent mosaics during their excavations, but took most of them to Rhodes in order to decorate the Grand Master's Palace (see page 46).

The most notable sculptures include a small statuette of Marsyas being punished by Apollo, a copy of the famous many-breasted Artemis of Ephesus, the expressive head of a dying warrior and the giant statue of a thinker, taken to be Hippocrates. (The museum is closed on Tuesdays.)

Excavations around the harbour
Through a gate on the east side of Eleftherias Square, Porta tou Forou,

you reach Porfiriou, a small street which runs parallel to the excavated area. You can relax here in pleasant bars and cafés before or after your visit. Here too is the entrance to the ancient town which is referred to simply as the *Agora*.

The excavated area is exceptionally confusing, but impressive because of its sheer size. The actual agora (market hall) was provided with an immense colonnaded hall 150 m long and 82 m wide. Only ruins remain of this stoa, the ancient town wall, the temples, shops and houses and an early Christian basilica, as the island was hit by devastating earthquakes in A.D. 142, 469 and 554. The expert can attempt to identify ruins from nine centuries; the layman will probably be satisfied to walk around the site.

Hippocrates' Plane-Tree Square (e)
At the north end of the Agora lies Plane-Tree Square, named after a gigantic plane-tree under which

Hippocrates is alleged to have taught. This is not very likely, but the lovingly supported plane-tree is undoubtedly one of the oldest trees in Europe. There is also a Turkish *fountain* where the water flows into an ancient sarcophagus, and the Mosque of Gazi Hasan Pasha (1786) (**f**), now closed.

The castle

From Plane-Tree Square you cross a bridge spanning the moat of the formidable Castle of the Knights, which dominates the town and harbour.

After the 4th Crusade (1204) the Dodecanese islands came under the control of various masters, ending with the Knights of St John who conquered Rhodes in 1309 and Kos in 1314. Faced with Turkish expansion they began the construction of this huge castle in 1391 and desperately carried on building for centuries — ultimately all in vain. As soon as the Turks conquered Rhodes

in 1522 the knights had also to abandon the outpost of Kos.

The walls of the building have been skilfully restored and you can walk along them during the museum's opening times. They offer marvellous views of the town and harbour.

Excavations in the south-west of the town

These lie between Grigoriou Street and Theologou Street and were only uncovered after the earthquake in 1933 (see map, page 75).

If you enter the site from Grigoriou Street, near Anapafseos Street (**1**), you first come to the *Decumana* (**2**) which runs parallel to Grigoriou Street and which is a splendid thoroughfare, dating from the 3rd c. A.D. On the right was the ancient acropolis, where a lonely minaret now stands. Below are several poorly preserved, and only roughly protected, *houses* (**3**), (**4**), (**5**), some decorated with frescos and

The plane-tree

The castle, Kos

others with mosaics. The most priceless of these is without doubt 'Europa and the Bull' (**5**), thought to be of 2nd c. origin. The Phoenician princess who gave her name to the continent of Europe is evidently not afraid of Zeus in the guise of a bull. More surprised than frightened, she lies naked across the back of the covetous bull-god who is to carry her off to Crete.

Further to the west you come to the area which has been much better excavated and which is bisected by a *road* running north-south (**6**). The most interesting remains are the *baths*, above which a *basilica* (**7**) was erected; the font and parts of the chancel have been preserved. Also to be seen are the public lavatories and the huge *gymnasion* (*xystos*) (**8**), with seventeen of the original eighty-one Doric columns rebuilt. In close proximity to the gymnasion are more large *baths* (**9**) and on the other side of the street a *forum* (**10**) with remains of a *stoa* (**11**).

At the north end of the site are some roofed houses; these contain valuable mosaics, which, however, are covered in sand to protect them. Of the many houses and shops only the foundations can be recognised.

Casa Romana (g)

To the east of Anapafseos Street, in the south-west part of the town and not far from the entrance to the excavations, is the Casa Romana (opening times as for the museum). Externally it looks an insignificant building but it is one which you should visit. A Roman villa of the 3rd c. A.D. which has been reconstructed illustrates the luxury with which the wealthy Romans surrounded themselves. They valued beautiful Kos because of its pleasant climate and its easy-going way of life. Whereas only scattered foundations remain from most of the houses on Kos, here you can form a vivid picture of how the Romans really lived. The extensive building is constructed around some open courtyards (atria) decorated with magnificent mosaics. Ruins of extensive baths can be seen in front of the Casa Romana.

Roman Odeion (h)

The Roman odeion is situated in Grigoriou Street, to the west. Nowadays musical and theatrical performances take place on this site, which has been heavily restored by the Italians, and which in ancient times served as a stage for oratory. During the Hellenistic period Kos had three other theatres, and although they are not worth visiting they indicate how prosperous and lively life in the town must have been.

Asklepieion (Sanctuary of Asklepios)

The Asklepieion is situated about 4 km south of Kos town on a pine-covered hill and stretches over three terraces. It is best reached from the town along Grigoriou Street. Just beyond the outskirts of the town you come to *Platani* which is chiefly inhabited by Turks. It is named after two enormous plane-trees which provide shade. A cypress-lined avenue leads past an international institute to the sanctuary.

The Asklepieion is the archaeological showpiece of Kos and for centuries was one of the main sources of its wealth. Apart from Epidauros Kos was the most famous sanctuary of Asklepios in the

Excavations in the south-west of the town

1. Entrance
2. Decumana
3. Block of houses
4. Block of houses
5. Block of houses
   House with mosaic of Europa
6. North-South street
7. Basilica
8. Gymnasion (Xystos)
9. Large baths
10. Forum
11. Stoa

50m

ancient world. The cult of Asklepios was probably brought to the island by the Doric immigrants in the 9th c. However, it did not attain real importance until the 5th c. and above all the 4th c., and it is no coincidence that the life and works of the famous doctor Hippocrates (460–377 B.C.) belonged to this time. Both names have associations which live on today. Doctors still acknowledge the Aesculapian staff as a symbol of their profession and are bound by the Hippocratic oath.

Asklepios was honoured as the son of Apollo and is supposed to have learnt the art of healing from the wise centaur Chiron. This is a clear indication that medicine was regarded not as a purely scientific discipline but rather as an art; what the priest-doctors were practising in the Asklepios sanctuaries — which were also sizeable sanatoria — was precisely that which has been rediscovered today as psychosomatic medicine — the treatment of body *and* soul. The god appeared to the sufferer in a dream and gave the instructions for

The Asklepieion, Kos

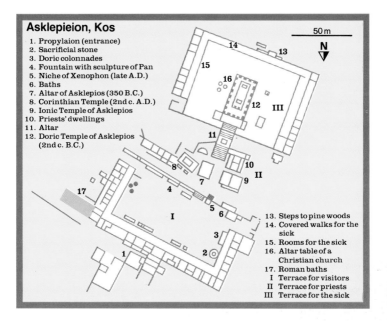

Asklepieion, Kos

1. Propylaion (entrance)
2. Sacrificial stone
3. Doric colonnades
4. Fountain with sculpture of Pan
5. Niche of Xenophon (late A.D.)
6. Baths
7. Altar of Asklepios (350 B.C.)
8. Corinthian Temple (2nd c. A.D.)
9. Ionic Temple of Asklepios
10. Priests' dwellings
11. Altar
12. Doric Temple of Asklepios (2nd c. B.C.)

13. Steps to pine woods
14. Covered walks for the sick
15. Rooms for the sick
16. Altar table of a Christian church
17. Roman baths
I   Terrace for visitors
II   Terrace for priests
III Terrace for the sick

50 m

recovery. It is clear that the experienced priest-doctors interpreted the dreams and based their therapy on them — together with the organic diagnosis.

They called themselves Asklepiads, descendants of Asklepios. The most famous of them was Hippocrates, who is regarded as the father of western medicine, and his basic demands are still valid today: accurate observation of human nature, exact description of the symptoms of the illness and strictly logical conclusions. Thus Hippocrates complemented the psychotherapeutic method of healing with scientific thinking and reliable empirical knowledge.

As already stated, the Hippocratic oath is named after him or at least after his school. After a preamble which illustrates the special status of doctors even in antiquity, there follow the crucial demands which were sworn before all the gods and goddesses.

'I shall apply dietary measures for the benefit of the sick according to my ability. Should they be threatened with danger and injury then I shall try to protect them. Neither shall I prescribe a fatal medicine, even if begged to do so, nor give advice along such lines. Similarly, I shall not assist any woman with the means of abortion. Purely and piously shall I live my life and practise my medicine. Into all the houses I enter I shall seek to bring benefit to the patients and avoid all deliberate and damaging wrong-doing. I shall remain silent about what I see or hear during the treatment and keep it secret.'

The whole archaeological site is essentially of 3rd c. B.C. origin. Festivals took place on the lowest terrace (another similarity with Epidauros). The large brick buildings

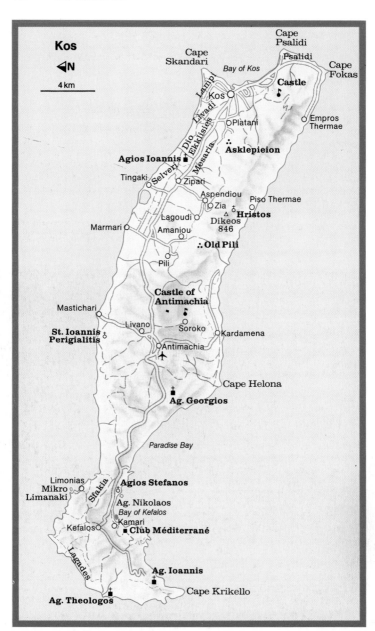

on the left-hand side are Roman baths. The terrace is enclosed by a wall with niches where statues of gods and votive images were displayed. On the left near the steps to the second terrace is a fountain with a sculpture of Pan. The second terrace was the actual level of the temples; the altar of Asklepios stood in the centre (350 B.C.), and next to it were a Corinthian temple and the Temple of Asklepios in Ionic style, as well as houses for the priests. Another flight of steps leads to the third terrace which commands a splendid view over Cape Skandari and the Bay of Kos. The Doric Temple of Asklepios, dating from the 2nd c., is situated here (in Christian times it was converted into a church of the Madonna), and around it are buildings and colonnaded halls for the sick. The Asklepieion was discovered in 1901 by R. Herzog and J. Zarraffis. The restoration dates from the Italian period.

Evenings out

Restaurants: *Château*, Eleftherias Square; *Chevalier*, Vas. Georgiou 4; *Platon*, Arseniou 3; *Faro*, near the lighthouse; *Bristol*, Vas. Georgiou 6; *13 Restaurant*, Artemissias 9a; *Gorgona*, near Dolphin Square.

Tavernas

It is necessary to search for these; often the most insignificant-looking ones are

Best-quality sponges on sale in the islands

best. Here is a selection: *Harama*, Kanar/Porfiriou St.; *Iviscos*, end of Vas. Georgiou St.; *Platanos*, Hippocrates' Plane-Tree Square; *Mavromatis*, Psalidi; *Drossia*, Nafklirou/corner of Alexandrou; *Anatolia Hamam*, Apellou, Old Town. The tavernas at Tingaki, Marmari, Mastichari and Kardamena specialise in fish and seafood.

♫ Discothèques:

Heaven, Zouroudi St. 5; *Cailua*, Zouroudi St. 5; *Playboy*, Dolphin Square, near the harbour; *Night Club* with bouzouki music, Hellas, 3 km outside the town.

A Tour of the Island

Leave Kos and head south along the road to Antimachia and the airport. After about 12 km, shortly beyond Zipari, there is a right turn to *Tingaki* which has an extensive beach and good tavernas. You can spend a restful day on the beach here; as the road is almost flat Tingaki is easily reached by bicycle. Just before Antimachia you turn off and soon come to *Mastichari*, a small resort with a sandy bay, several tavernas and a lovely view of the island of Kalymnos.

Continuing on the main road, just before you reach Antimachia a small signposted road leads to *Antimachia Castle* (14th–15th c.), the second large knights' castle. It is not nearly as well preserved as the harbour castle and has not been restored but its size is impressive. If you enjoy romantic ruins you should not miss this diversion. Antimachia is only of significance for tourists because this is where Kos's new airport is situated. Continue along the main road towards Kefalos.

After a further 10 km a road on the left leads to the sea and a magnificent sandy beach which is aptly named *Paradise*. The road gets closer to the coast and after a few kilometres you can see the immense hotel complex of the *Club Méditerranée*. Here you should turn left because not far from the hotel are the ruins of two early Christian basilicas built one inside the other, *Agios Stefanos*. The ruins of Agios Stefanos are the best-preserved of early Christian churches on Kos and are worth a visit for this reason alone. Unfortunately the floor mosaics are not visible; they have been covered with a layer of sand to protect them.

From Agios Stefanos you have a lovely view of the little island lying opposite, *Agios Nikolaos,* and Kefalos Bay with its beautiful beach. In the mountain village of *Kefalos* can be seen the only windmill still working on Kos. Below Kefalos on a sandy bay lies the fishing hamlet of *Kamari* with some pretty tavernas. Organised excursions finish at Kefalos. If you wish to see the virtually uninhabited southernmost part of the island then hire a jeep for the roads are still quite rough. Apart from deserted coves there are the churches of St John (Agios Ioannis) and John the Theologian (Agios Theologos) standing in complete isolation. They were founded by the Blessed Christodoulos, who later built the monastery of St John on Patmos.

A little to the south of Kefalos a few ruins indicate that Astypalaia once stood here; it was the biggest town on the island before the founding of Kos as the capital. Return to Antimachia from where you can visit *Kardamena* to the east, a fishing village which has developed in recent years into a seaside resort geared to tourists. Along unmetalled but scenically delightful roads you can drive from Kardamena to *Pili*; near the entrance to this rebuilt village you can visit the *Charmyleion*, a type of ancient crypt dedicated to a hero of the same name of whom little is known. The Stavros church is built over it. You can drive through Pili to Amaniou and from there walk to *Old Pili*

(Palaiopili), an uninhabited town, where you will find three early Byzantine churches with well preserved frescos, and the ruins of the former castle. From Pili (or more easily and on a better road from Zipari) you can continue to the picturesque mountain villages Aspendiou, Lagoudi and Zia. The highest mountain on the island, the 846-m-high Dikeos, with its superb views, is accessible from Zia.

Travelling east from the capital there are hotels, restaurants and tavernas practically all the way to Cape Psalidi. The road runs almost parallel to the beach which is a mixture of pebbles and sand. Then all becomes deserted as far as *Cape Fokas*, where there is a sandy cove (and the Hotel Dimitrias) as well as lovely views of the Turkish Knidos Peninsula. After Fokas the route becomes steep and winding. Shortly before the road ends a sandy track leads down to a lovely cove which is called *Empros Thermae* on account of a small medicinal spring. There are facilities for bathing, and a taverna.

The windmill at Kefalos

🚌 Excursions from Kos
Kos is ideally suited for day trips to the surrounding islands.

Rhodes
This can be reached in two hours by hydrofoil.

Patmos
The holy island of the Orthodox Church, with a splendid fortified *monastery* founded in the 11th c. by the Blessed Christodoulos from Kos, also has a picturesque *chora* nestling around the monastery, and the grotto in which St John is said to have written the Apocalypse.

Leros
There is a mighty fortress here dating from the time of the Knights of St John. During both world wars the island was an important naval base. Today the largest psychiatric hospital in Greece is situated on the island.

Bodrum
This town (pop. 8000) on the Turkish coast opposite is similarly easy to get to, unless excursions by boat are prohibited on political or economic grounds. Bodrum (the ancient Halikarnassos) has itself become a not inconsiderable holiday centre. Its lively bazaars are impressive. The principal sights are the castle of the Knights of St John by the harbour, the Archaeological Museum, the ancient theatre and the remains of the old town walls. Virtually nothing remains of the Mausoleum, one of the seven wonders of the ancient world; a model of it can be seen in the museum.

Day excursions from Kos can be made to Pserimos, Kalymnos and Nisyros. Regular boat services ply to Tilos, Astypalaia and Symi, but trips to these islands necessitate spending a night there. All these islands are described below.

The neighbouring islands

Kos and Rhodes are the two most heavily populated islands in the Dodecanese and the most important from the point of view of tourism. However, all the other sixteen islands in the archipelago are worth visiting. Below, in alphabetical order, are brief descriptions of eleven of them.

Astypalaia Pop. 1100, area 97 sq. km

Astypalaia is the link between the archipelagos of the Cyclades and the Dodecanese. It lies approximately halfway between Amorgos and Kos. Few tourists come here outside the main summer months. The island's port, *Skala*, with its small hotels and tavernas, has become merged with *Chora*, the medieval capital. Chora is situated on a 100-m-high hill, together with a castle of the Knights of St John. Architecturally it has more in common with the Cyclades than with the Dodecanese. To the west of this main residential area is the green valley of Livadia, by the sea. Two other hamlets are *Vathi*, in the north-east of the island, and *Analipsi*, which is also known as Martizana. The best beaches are on the 60-m-wide tongue of land which joins the eastern and western parts of the island. Much of Astypalaia lacks roads and is best explored on foot. Day excursions are run to the island from Kos and Kalymnos, but visitors from Rhodes must make their own travel arrangements and will have to spend several nights on the island.

Chalki Pop. 380, area 28 sq.km

Chalki is a bare island and the inhabitants earn their living almost exclusively from stock farming and fishing. The fish is sold to restaurants in Rhodes. The beach is ten minutes' walk from the only village on the island. Accommodation is available in private pensions and houses. Tourists can visit Chalki from Rhodes, either from Rhodes town or from Kamiros-Skala,

but they must make their own arrangements and it will almost always be necessary to spend a night on the island. Day excursions by hydrofoil are operated from Kos.

Kalymnos Pop. 13,200, area 111 sq. km

Kalymnos is the only Greek island which still maintains a commercially viable trade in sponge fishing. Each year just after Easter about 300 inhabitants leave the island in their small caïques to dive for sponges in the Aegean and in other parts of the Mediterranean. When they return in September or October their catch of thousands of sponges is laid out to dry on the streets of *Pothia*, the island's capital. Pothia is a lively town and, unlike Rhodes and Kos, has not yet been overrun by tourists. Italian administrative buildings by the harbour, and prosperous-looking houses with limewashed walls in pastel colours, are impressive features of the townscape. The houses are set picturesquely in tiers on the slopes behind the town. A level valley extends from Pothia to the west coast of the island. In this valley lies *Chora*, the medieval island capital, which is still a thriving place. Above Chora rises a steep hill which is strewn with the ruins of churches and with chapels; on the rocky summit àre the remains of a medieval castle. *Kandouni, Mirties* and *Massouri*, the seaside resorts of Kalymnos, are situated on the west coast. As they are sheltered from the open sea by the island of Telendos, the scenery, with its numerous fruit-trees

Church architecture, Kalymnos

and cypresses, is reminiscent of that of the North Italian lakes. Visitors who prefer a very quiet seaside resort are recommended to try *Emborio* in the extreme north-east.

There is an attractive excursion from Pothia into the luxuriant valley of *Vathi*, with many orange and mandarin groves. The village itself lies at the far end of a narrow fjord, almost 2 km long, cut into the rock; bathing is possible here. The south of the island is also worth visiting. There are three 20th c. monasteries here, to which visitors are welcome, *Agia Ekaterinis*, *Agion Pandon* and *Evangelistrias*, as well as

Pothia, Kalymnos

the hamlet of *Vothini* with attractive tavernas and a shady beach.

Day excursions to Kalymnos are run from Kos, but visitors from Rhodes must be prepared to spend at least one night on the island.

Karpathos Pop. 5400, area 301 sq. km

Although Karpathos is somewhat larger than Kos, it has only a quarter as many inhabitants. The island is extremely hilly and still has comparatively poor communications. Many more traditions have survived on Karpathos than elsewhere. Since 1988 tourism has become significant only in *Pigadhia*, the island capital. Pigadhia has a good sandy beach, a modern church with a completely painted interior, and, on the edge of the township, the ruins of an early Christian basilica by the sea.

The hill villages in the hinterland of Pigadhia, including *Menetes, Aperi, Volada, Othos* and *Piles*, are quite unspoilt. The remains of another early Christian basilica, with a beautiful mosaic floor, can be seen near *Arkassa*, a village with a good beach on the east coast. *Diafani*, in the northern half of the island, has a harbour, but there is only a single unmetalled road leading to this area. High above the west coast is the large village of *Olimbos*, which clings to its traditions more strongly than any other village on the Greek islands. Most of the women here wear their traditional costume every day, and on feast days everybody dresses in festival attire. Visits are recommended during Holy Week and at Easter. Karpathos can be reached from Rhodes by ferry or by air. Although a day's excursion by air is possible, visitors are recommended to spend at least one night on the island.

Kassos Pop. 1000, area 9 sq.km

Kassos forms the link between the Dodecanese and Crete. From the sea the little island appears completely bare and stony. The capital and port is *Fry* which seems less commercialised than any other island capital in Greece; the island therefore attracts very few visitors from abroad. It is ideal for anyone who likes to spend his holiday among Greeks and who can do without a beach — for Kassos has none. If you wander along the only inhabited valley, in which Fry is situated, you will realise that the vegetation on the island lies hidden behind the numerous walls, and that is why it cannot be seen from the sea. The people of Kassos are very friendly and this compensates for their less than picturesque villages. Kassos can be reached from Rhodes by ferry or by plane. In either case it is necessary to spend at least one night on the island.

Kastellorizo Pop. 220, area 9 sq. km

The most easterly Greek island, also called *Megisti*, Kastellorizo lies 130 km from Rhodes, immediately off the little Turkish coastal town of Kas. Along the shore and in the hilly streets of the only village on the island stand hundreds of mainly two-storeyed houses. Vines and fig-trees are growing out of some of them, and almost all the doors and windows are closed. Fifty years ago Kastellorizo had 14,000 inhabitants but after the war nearly all of them emigrated to Australia. However, most of the emigrants arranged for their houses to be looked after, so that Kastellorizo is not a completely unattractive place. By the harbour stands a fort, housing a small archaeological and folklore museum. On a hill behind the village can be seen the remains of a medieval settlement and castle. Visitors can take a boat trip to a charming grotto, and swim in the clear water of the harbour basin, which is overlooked by the Taurus mountains. You can get to Kastellorizo by plane or ship from Rhodes, but a night has to be spent on the island.

Nisyros Pop. 1250, area 41 sq. km
The Acropolis of Athens is a masterpiece of man; Nisyros is a masterpiece of nature, one of the great sights of Greece. The island is a completely intact volcano. The verdant slopes which rise from the Aegean form not the usual mountain summits and hilltops, but the rim of a crater. This drops more than 500 m into a huge, basin-shaped valley (caldera) which is over 3½ km in diameter. Half of it is green pasture; the rest looks like a bare lunar landscape, with craters and little volcanic cones. On the rim of the crater are the two almost uninhabited ghost villages of *Nikia* and *Emborio*. In and between the two ports of *Mandraki* and *Pali* are several hotels and the bathing facilities of *Lutra* which are provided with hot water from the volcano. In Mandraki you can visit the remains of a small castle of the Knights of St John. Just outside the village can be seen one of the best-preserved town walls in Greece (5th–4th c. B.C.). From Kos town and Kardamena (Kos) there are day excursions by hydrofoil to Nisyros. Visitors from Rhodes usually have to spend at least one night on the island.

Pserimos Pop. 100, area 17 sq.km
The tiny island of Pserimos does not even have an electricity power plant; current for the tavernas and houses is provided by private generators. The inhabitants earn their living by stock farming and fishing, and they supplement their income by catering for the day excursionists from Kos and Kalymnos. The island has a good beach and overnight accommodation.

Symi Pop. 2400, area 58 sq. km
Most visitors to Rhodes make a day excursion to Symi. The crossing to this island, which consists of karst limestone, takes about two hours. Symi is also the name of the principal township and harbour where visitors arrive. Its houses are picturesquely situated in the hilly countryside. Formerly most of the inhabitants earned their living by fishing and sponge-fishing, but from ancient times until quite recently the island was also well known for shipbuilding. Today most Symiots live abroad; the majority

Volcanic landscape of Nisyros

Symi

of the present islanders are fishermen or they cater for tourists, for on Symi, in addition to rooms in the few hotels, there are numerous villas for rent. You can get to the 12th c. *Panormitis Monastery* either by boat or on foot. Since the 18th c. the monastery has been a popular place of pilgrimage. The impressive buildings, which include a substantial guest-wing, are situated right on the shore. A fine carved wooden iconostasis, with an icon of St

Michael, and well preserved frescos are noteworthy. The library should not be missed, for it contains valuable manuscripts, jewellery and paintings. A speciality of the monastery is an unusual fig liqueur. Day excursions by hydrofoil are occasionally run to Symi from Kos.

Telendos Pop. 50, area 5 sq. km
This tiny island off Mirties on the west coast of Kalymnos is only five minutes

away by boat (several times daily). Private apartments are available, and the best bathing is to be had from a beach on the east coast, a short distance from the only village. The inhabitants earn their living by fishing.

Tilos Pop. 500, area 63 sq. km
This sparsely populated island, with two villages, small beaches, seven ruined castles, and mountains up to 651 m in height, is an ideal destination for those who prefer a quiet place for a walking holiday. One interesting walk of 10 km from the main village is to the *Monastery of St Panteleimon*, where you can spend the night.

Day excursions to Tilos are not possible. To best appreciate the beauty of the island you need at least two days. Ferries from Kos and Rhodes provide opportunities for an extended visit.

Useful things to know

Before you go
Climate
Rhodes and Kos are called 'islands of the sun' with good reason. The sun shines almost uninterruptedly every day from May until October, so that the islands get about 3250 hours of sunshine a year, but even in high summer it is not unbearably hot because the *Meltemi*, a north-west wind, provides a pleasant, continual cool breeze.

What to take
On Rhodes and Kos you can obtain nearly everything you might need on holiday, but it is advisable to take anything that you particularly require, as many articles, such as films and cosmetics, are more expensive in Greece. Good sunglasses are essential and it is important to take sufficient suntan cream – the effect of the sun is not always noticed because of the cool breeze.

Clothing should be light and comfortable. Formal attire is not required, but in the larger hotels you are not expected to appear for dinner dressed in beachwear. As some of the coves are rocky and may contain spiky sea urchins, bathing shoes are useful. There is no need to take diving masks, flippers and snorkels as these can all be bought on Rhodes at prices similar to those at home. Stout comfortable footwear is recommended for those who intend to do much walking.

First-aid kit. Most common international medicines are available on Rhodes and Kos, but it is advisable to take a small first-aid kit with you. It should contain a pain-killer, treatment for stomach and digestive upsets, headache tablets, and something for colds. Also take an antiseptic and plasters for minor wounds. You should, of course, take any medicines that have been prescribed for you or that you take regularly.

Insurance
Although as citizens of the European Community British visitors are entitled to medical treatment equivalent to that provided for the Greeks, it is nevertheless advisable to take out private health insurance for the duration of the holiday, including cover for a flight home in an emergency. To obtain benefit under EC agreements it is essential for a UK national to be in possession of form E 111 obtainable from the DSS; an application form is obtainable from DSS offices or from main post offices.

Getting to Rhodes and Kos
By Air: Rhodes and Kos both have good airports. There are flights from Athens but most visitors on package holidays travel on charter flights from UK airports.

The luggage allowance on charter flights (20 kg) cannot be exceeded. Excess baggage is not allowed even against payment. Coats, cameras, binoculars and books for the journey may be carried as hand luggage. Excess baggage is permitted on scheduled and private flights but it is expensive. If you are travelling independently, you have to transfer from the international airport in Athens by bus or taxi to the Olympic Airways airport, where your luggage has to be checked in again.

On Rhodes the distance from the airport to Rhodes town is 18 km; on Kos the distance from the airport to Kos town is 14 km. Transport is by bus or taxi. On package tours transfers from the airport are arranged.

By sea: There are ferries from Piraeus to Rhodes and Kos, and you can reach the surrounding islands by ferry or hydrofoil.

Immigration and customs

Passports. Holders of a valid British passport can visit Greece for up to three months without a visa.

Entry. Personal effects required during the holiday and gifts of limited value may be taken into the islands duty-free. Equipment of a high value must be recorded in the owner's passport on arrival to ensure its export without difficulty.

The usual duty-free allowances common in the EC apply to Greece. These are: 300 cigarettes or 150 cigarillos or 75 cigars or 400 gr. tobacco; 5 litres wine and 3 litres spirits below 22% or 1.5 litres spirits over 22%. If purchased on an aircraft or in a duty-free shop these quantities are reduced by approximately one third. These concessions apply only to visitors who are seventeen years of age and over. The import of Greek currency is limited to 200,000 drachmas.

Exit. A limit of 25,000 drachmas may be taken out, together with other currency not exceeding the equivalent of 1000 U.S. dollars, provided it was declared upon entry. The duty-free allowances on re-entry into Great Britain are the same as those given above.

During your stay

Currency

The basic unit of Greek currency is the drachma. The rate of exchange varies from day to day but is the same at all banks and post offices. It is normally better to change money in Greece than in the UK, taking just enough for use on arrival.

Cash, travellers' cheques and Eurocheques can be changed at banks and post offices. Eurocheques must be made out in drachmas (maximum 25,000 Drs. per cheque). Credit cards are fairly widely accepted. Cash can be obtained at the National Bank for Eurocard and Visa, and at the Commercial Bank for Diners Club card.

Chemists

A Greek chemist's shop is called a **ΦAPMAKEION** (Farmakion) and is recognisable by a red or green Maltese cross on a white background. English is generally understood.

Electricity

The current on Rhodes and Kos is 220v AC. A Continental adaptor is necessary for electric razors etc.

Health

It is probably better for a visitor to pay any doctor's fees in cash and claim a refund on return home (see Insurance). Hotel management or the tour company will gladly be of assistance in an emergency and make the necessary arrangements.

Information in English

The excellent magazine 'Where and How' contains general information in English, German and Swedish. Radio news bulletins in English are transmitted daily at 7.30 a.m. Greek time.

Opening times

Banks: Monday to Friday 8 a.m.–2 p.m.

Chemists: Generally open from 8.30 a.m.–1.30 or 2 p.m.; on Sunday also from 5–8 p.m.

Museums: Museums in Greece are generally closed on Tuesdays. The opening times of museums and archaeological sites change so frequently that it is best to check beforehand. (Information from hotels, tour companies and EOT.)

Post and telephone offices: See entry

Shops and offices: Shops are generally open from 8 a.m.–1 p.m. and 5–8 p.m.; administrative offices only in the morning. All shops and offices are closed on Wednesday afternoon; only souvenir shops open on Sunday afternoon.

Photography
Cameras without tripods may be used in museums and on archaeological sites on payment of a fee. Special permission is required to photograph and film with tripods (and/or flash). This must be applied for in good time from branches of the Ministry of Ancient Monuments (*Efories Klassikon* and *Byzantinon Archaiotiton*) in Athens or from the appropriate Eforia in Rhodes (Street of the Knights).

Post offices
Post offices are open on Monday to Friday from 8 a.m.–8 p.m. Surface mail takes a long time, and visitors are recommended to send all letters by air.

Public holidays
See Festivals and Events in Rhodes (pages 41, 42).

Telephone
The Telephone and Telegraph Office (O.T.E.) is open on Monday to Friday from 8 a.m.–midnight, and on Saturday from 8 a.m.–4 p.m. For Britain dial 00 44, the area code without the initial 0, and the number.

Tipping
Tips are, of course, expected, as they are anywhere else in the world, and they certainly make life easier for the visitor. In the case of package tours it should not be assumed that tips are included in the cost. Good service and courtesy should be rewarded by a tip over and above the inclusive price; 10% of a bill is customary. You cannot take it for granted that the service charges included in the total holiday price are passed on to the staff by the hoteliers. The staff are mostly employed only during the season, and often have to live for the whole year on what they earn in four or five months.

Transport in the islands
Buses are the only means of public transport on Rhodes and Kos but they are very reliable. They stop everywhere in the capitals and at all important places on the islands. However, it is not always possible to return the same day from the more remote villages on the islands, as the buses remain at their destination overnight. Local travel agencies arrange excursions, with English speaking guides, to popular destinations.

Car Hire: Cars can be hired from the international and regional agencies. (Hotels and tour companies are also helpful). A national driving licence is all that is required. International traffic regulations apply in Greece but you must always be prepared for sudden flocks of sheep, horse-drawn carts or moped riders pulling out. Be especially careful at night. Comprehensive insurance is strongly recommended. Before setting out check the steering, tyres, brakes and lights. For shorter journeys bicycles can be hired in most towns.

Taxis: Many of the less well known but interesting places on the islands can only be reached by taxi or hired car. For longer journeys by taxi you should agree the price beforehand, if necessary with the help of a hotel receptionist.

Important addresses

National Tourist Organisation of Greece
195–197 Regent Street,
London W1R 8DL;
tel. (01) 734 5997.

In Greece

British Embassy
Odos Ploutarkhou 1,
Athens;
tel. (01) 7 23 62 11.

British Consulate
Odos 23 Martio 23,
Rhodes;
tel. (0241) 2 72 47 and 2 73 06.

Greek National Tourist Office (E.O.T.)
Arch. Makariou 5 and Papagou Street,
Rhodes;
tel. (0241) 2 36 55 and 2 32 55.

Right: Turkish Mosque, Rhodes
Below: Lindos

92

Useful Words and Phrases

Although English is understood in the islands, the visitor will undoubtedly find a few words and phrases of Greek very useful. There is no standard system of transliteration of the Greek alphabet into Roman script. In the examples given below an approximate pronunciation only is given. In modern Greek the stress on a word of more than one syllable is always shown by an accent.

The Greek alphabet

A	α	Alpha	I	ι	Iota	P	ρ	Rho
B	β	Beta	K	κ	Kappa	Σ	σ	Sigma
Γ	γ	Gamma	Λ	λ	Lambda	T	τ	Tau
Δ	δ	Delta	M	μ	Mu	Y	υ	Upsilon
E	ε	Epsilon	N	ν	Nu	Φ	φ	Phi
Z	ζ	Zeta	Ξ	ξ	Xi	X	χ	Chi
H	η	Eta	O	o	Omicron	Ψ	ψ	Psi
Θ	θ	Theta	Π	π	Pi	Ω	ω	Omega

Ruins at the Acropolis, Lindos

In the pronunciation guide below the following should be noted:
dh = th in *this*; th = th in *thick*; kh = approximately the sound of ch in the Scottish word *loch*. Greek uses a semi-colon for a question mark.

please	parakaló	free	eléftheros
thank you	efkharistó	entrance	isodhós
yes/no	ne *or* málista/óchie	exit	eksodhós
excuse me	me sinkhoríte	today / tomorrow	símera / ávrio
do you speak English?	omelíte angliká?	Sunday / Monday	kiriakí / dheftéra
I do not understand	dhem katalamvéno	Tuesday / Wednesday	tríti / tetárti
good morning/	kaliméra	Thursday / Friday	pémpti / paraskeví
afternoon		Saturday / holiday	sávato / skholí
good evening	kalispéra		
good night	kaliníkhta		
good bye	adío		
how much?	póso káni?		
a single room	dhomátio mé éna kreváti		
a double room	dhomátio mé dhio krevátia		
with bath	mé bánio / lutró		
I should like	thaíthela		
the bill, please	to logariasmós parakaló		
everything included	óla simberilamvano-ménoo		
open / shut	aniktós / klistós		
where is ... street?	pu iné to i odhós?		
... square?	i platía?		

how far?	póso makhriá?	
left	aristerá	0 midhén
right	dheksiá	1 énas / éna
straight on	katefthían	2 dhío
post office	takhidhromío	3 tría
bank	trápesa	4 téssera
railway station	stathmós	5 pénde
exchange office	saráfiko	6 éksi
police station	astinomíkotmima	7 eftá
public telephone	tiléfono	8 okhtó
information office	grafíopliroforíon	9 ennéa
doctor	yatrós	10 dhéka
chemist	farmakío	11 éndheka
toilet	tooaléta	12 dódheka
ladies	yinekón	20 íkosi
gentlemen	andhrón	50 penínda
engaged	katiliménos	100 ekató

The meanings of names

On street signs and maps, and in the names of places, monasteries, churches, natural features, etc., the same words occur again and again. It is helpful for the visitor to know what these words signify and so a selection will be found below together with their English meanings.

Ágia	ΑΓΙΑ	saint (female)
Ágii	ΑΓΙΟΙ	saints
Ágios	ΑΓΙΟΣ	saint (male)
Akrotíri	ΑΚΡΩΤΗΡΙ	cape
Chóra	ΧΩΡΑ	island capital
Chorió	ΧΩΡΙΟ	village
Fáros	ΦΑΡΟΣ	lighthouse
Froúrio	ΦΡΟΥΡΙΟ	fortress/castle
Kástro	ΚΑΣΤΡΟ	fortress/castle
Kólpos	ΚΟΛΠΟΣ	bay
Leofóros	ΛΕΩΦΟΡΟΣ	boulevard/avenue
Limáni	ΛΙΜΑΝΙ	harbour
Límni	ΛΙΜΝΙ	lake/pond
Livádi	ΛΙΒΑΔΙ	meadow/pasture
Monastíri/Moní	ΜΟΝΑΣΤΗΡΙ/ΜΟΝΙ	monastery
Nisí/Nísos	ΝΗΣΙ/ΝΗΣΟΣ	island
Odós	ΟΔΟΣ	road/street
Órmos	ΟΡΜΟΣ	bay/anchorage
Óros	ΟΡΟΣ	mountain
Panagía	ΠΑΝΑΓΙΑ	Virgin Mary
Pantokrátor	ΠΑΝΤΟΚΡΑΤΩΡ	Ruler of the world/Christ
Paralía	ΠΑΡΑΛΙΑ	beach/shore
Pélagos	ΠΕΛΑΓΟΣ	sea
Platía	ΠΛΑΤΕΙΑ	square
Pólis	ΠΟΛΙΣ	town
Potámi/Potamós	ΠΟΤΑΜΙ/ΠΟΤΑΜΟΣ	river/stream
Spíleo	ΣΠΗΛΑΙΟ	cave
Stavrós	ΣΤΑΥΡΟΣ	cross/crossing
Vathí	ΒΑΘΗ	depth/background
Áno/Epáno	ΑΝΩ/ΕΠΑΝΩ	upper/over
Archéa	ΑΡΧΑΙΑ	ancient
Káto	ΚΑΤΩ	under/lower
Méga/Megálo	ΜΕΓΑ/ΜΕΓΑΛΟ	great
Paleó	ΠΑΛΑΙΟ	old

INDEX

Original German text: Wolf Seidl
English translation: Julie Waller
Series Editor – English edition: Alec Court.

Photography: Alan Boardman (pages 1, 11, 13, 19, 35, 38, 43, 52, 53 top, 57 left, 91, 92);
Andrew Hawkins (pages 14, 22, 45, 47, 55, 57 right, 60, 66, 86); Miss D. F. Goodrick (cover
and pages 3, 24, 27, 31, 49, 50, 62, 69, 70, 73, 74); Travel Trade Photography (pages 32, 67);
Pam Everitt (pages 10, 12)

The publishers have made every endeavour to ensure the accuracy of this publication but can
accept no responsibility for any errors or omissions. They would, however, appreciate
notification of any inaccuracies to correct future editions.

Printed in Italy

ISBN 0-7117-0474-0